THE 5 ESSENTIALS

The

Using Your Inborn Resources to Create a Fulfilling Life

5

ESSENTIALS

Bob Deutsch, PhD

with Lou Aronica

HUDSON
STREET
PRESS

HUDSON STREET PRESS
Published by the Penguin Group
Penguin Group (USA), 375 Hudson Street,
New York, New York 10014, USA

USA | Canada | UK | Ireland | Australia | New Zealand | India | South Africa | China
Penguin Books Ltd, Registered Offices: 80 Strand, London WC2R 0RL, England
For more information about the Penguin Group visit penguin.com

First published by Hudson Street Press, a member of Penguin Group (USA), 2013

REGISTERED TRADEMARK—MARCA REGISTRADA
HUDSON
STREET
PRESS

LIBRARY OF CONGRESS CATALOGING-IN-PUBLICATION DATA

Deutsch, Bob (Robert D.)
  The 5 essentials : using your inborn resources to create a fulfilling life / Dr. Bob
Deutsch, with Lou Aronica.
      pages cm
  Includes bibliographical references and index.
  ISBN 978-1-59463-122-1
  1. Success.   2. Self-realization.   3. Self-actualization (Psychology)   I. Aronica,
Lou.   II. Title.
  BF637.S8D42 2013
  158—dc23
                                                                      2013021130

Printed in the United States of America
10 9 8 7 6 5 4 3 2 1

Set in Warnock Pro
Designed by Eve L. Kirch

This book is dedicated to the memory of
Herman, Muriel, Pearl, Milton, and Molly.

Show us how genius deals with its own mistakes, and how normal, hardworking people can be surprised by bursts of creativity. Specify for us, in terms that touch our own experience, the exuberance and patience, the courage and humility, that allow creative people to break out through the boundaries of the past with each new thought.

—Robert Grudin, *The Grace of Great Things*

Contents

Part 2: The Five Key Processes

Acknowledgments

IN A SENSE I began writing this book at birth, even before I had language. It is my personal story reflected upon and then turned outward as a parable for everyone, to make of it whatever they will. Yes, my story—just like everyone's story—is unique. But if you look at your own life's narratives and the narratives that informed them, you can abstract certain universal principles. I have done that in hopes that others would be motivated to find their own story—what I call "self-story"—and use that to evoke their own ongoing self-expansion.

Many have helped me to consider and continue to create my own self-story. To all those unwitting coauthors I am indebted to you for my life—for what is a life other than the narratives that make up "I"?

The impetus for this book came as a result of a process I write about in these pages: directed serendipity. I have a plan, I start enacting that plan, then the plan meets up with the world, and I go careening off in this direction and that direction depending on my own mass and velocity, seeing what excites and attracts me or does not.

As a result of some writings I did, I once got a call to give a speech. Diane McArter, who was in that audience, later called and asked me to talk at an event she was organizing. It sounded interesting, so I agreed to participate. After that speech a man came over to me and introduced himself. His name is Peter Miller. Peter became my literary agent. He is good, in every sense of the word. He then introduced me to Lou Aronica, who helped me write this book. At Peter's behest I met Lou for breakfast one morning in New York, and before our oatmeal was served I already felt he was like a brother. We were simpatico in so many ways, and complementary in many others. My brain works by symbolic association and metaphor. That has its benefits (I hope), and it has its downside. Lou, by his graceful intelligence and book-producing skills, found a way to take my deficits and help make them artful. Regardless of what comes of this book, meeting Peter and Lou has already made writing it a success for me. These now buddies of mine helped me give voice to what was already in me but was loosely formed. They helped me expand myself. Also in the process of writing this book, Sydney Olshan provided research support that always showed initiative and intelligence, regardless of the difficulty of the research request. Her persistence consistently encouraged the feeling of forward motion in the writing pace. That's important.

Caroline Sutton, my editor, not only took on this project with enthusiasm, but after the first draft was completed, she made a recommendation that changed the structure of the book. I immediately knew her suggestion was right, and true, and necessary to make this book better than what was on the page at that moment. She pointed to the need to make the idea of self-story the fulcrum of *The 5 Essentials*. In doing so, Caroline Sutton became an everlasting part of my self-story.

Others, each by contributing in their unique way to my continuing search for my own way, prepared me for my eventual union with agent and cowriter.

Family first. After my father's early death at age thirty-five, my mother sacrificed much to see that I had plenty. My father, I am told, even at thirty-five, had already given me all he had to give: He was a dreamer; so am I. His sister, Molly, was also of that kind. Just by her way of being, she added to my dreaming. My mother's sister, Pearl, her husband, Milton, and their son, Martin, always looked out for me, especially when I most needed looking out for. I owe them so much. And as I suspect is not too uncommon in families, in addition to learning from our elders we gain from our youngers. My daughter (and only child), Phoebe, inspired me to do the opposite of what most new parents do: Because of her intrinsic joy, she made me *less* responsible. Her happiness, positive expectations, and playfulness made me discover the deeper dreamer in me. For that, she was "parent" to me. She remains a total joy. Kathy Drasher, my wife now of seven years, has stimulated a journey we have taken together that has been fun, especially in the midst of the hopscotch directions we have traveled to find a home in a place we both love. She has also taught me about beauty. She *is* it and she has an eye for it. Her artistry captures my attention on a daily basis.

Many colleagues and friends have also been crucial in my life. Albert Scheflen and Robert Plutchik, at Albert Einstein College of Medicine, first helped me thwack out a career path that excited and challenged me. Ada Reif Esser then taught me something about how to add depth to that path. She often read me the riot act, and I trusted her enough to take her admonitions to heart. She is still with me in my heart. Next I met Lionel Tiger, the Charles Darwin professor of anthropology and sociology at Rutgers. His brilliance, gentlemanly manner, and fierce commitment to truth and to mankind continue to influence me. Lionel indirectly guided me to all manner of things that eventually led me to the Max Planck Institute in Seewiesen, Germany, and to Dr. Iraneus Eibl-Eibesfeldt, Nobel Laureate Konrad Lorenz, and Dr. Wulf Schiefenhovel. My years working with them and under the auspices of the institute were vital to my developing self-story. These three bighearted men gave me the gift of showing me that science and the artistry of science could be made one. They helped me find me.

George Scribner, first a colleague and very soon thereafter a friend, has it all, a softness that can be strong, and a feeling for the everyday life of people that is as genuine as it is insightful. I value him greatly. I was introduced to Tom McCaffery by someone who wanted to hire me as a consultant, but before she would, she said I would have to "get through" Tom. Well, I don't know if I got through Tom, but he sure got to me. He got to me as someone who is doing justice to what is and what could be. He is someone to be reckoned with. And I reckon he is also now my friend. I take meeting Jeffrey Rayport as an example of how the seeming chaos of the cosmos can work directly for one's betterment. A decade before I met Jeffrey, someone I was working with introduced me to someone else, who introduced me to Jeffrey. Jeffrey is singular: the best a friend can be and the best a brain can be. I adore him. I met Michael Spiessbach through a fleeting encounter I had with a mutual acquaintance. These many years later I still think of Michael the same way I did after our first meeting—he's fun, knows about what comprises a life, is Mr. Curiosity, and stands as a living totem to personal integrity.

To all the people I interviewed for this book, some world renowned and some known only in their world, I owe a great deal. Each opened their hearts and minds to me, and in doing so, opened me. The audio recordings and printed transcripts I have of those sessions are to me nothing less than ritual incantations and sacred texts. To highlight just two I interviewed—Wynton Marsalis and Debra Byrd—their ways of being and their ways of expressing their being have no time tag. Their way is age-old and ageless, wise.

Two other people I quoted in this book had a similarly huge effect on me: Paul Simon and Bruce Springsteen. Paul Simon speaks eloquently about collaboration when talking about the making of his award-winning album *Graceland*. His way of fusing impulses from different cultures into a singular vision that retains the authenticity of each contribution stands as a model for every person and every nation, if we ever are going to stop "tumbling into turmoil" and see more peaceful and brighter days. Bruce Springsteen . . . well, I now know why he's "the Boss." This man is living a totally conscious life, conscious of his own and others' courage and frailties, and conscious of his responsibilities to himself and to his audience. He's the benevolent leader humankind has always hoped and waited for.

All these people helped me dream. All these people are a lasting part of my self-story. They are essential.

Introduction

WHO ARE YOUR favorite characters from novels? My guess is that even if you don't read much fiction, you have a few. Maybe it's Jane Eyre because she's so strong. Or Huck Finn because he's so crafty. Perhaps it's Hermione Granger, from the *Harry Potter* novels, because she's so smart and centered. Then again, it could be Sam-I-am, from *Green Eggs and Ham*, because he's so damned persistent. All of these characters resonate with us because they feel larger than life. They seem iconic, representing outsize versions of us. They have *great* stories.

Maybe you've considered characters like these from time to time and wondered what it would be like to have that kind of substance, that kind of consequence, to have that kind of effect on the world. What would it be like to live a life that has the impact and color of a great literary character?

Maybe it's time for you to find out. Because you have everything inside you necessary to have a great, meaningful, and *constantly alive* story—to be the Hermione or Huck in your world and in the worlds of the people around you. To contribute big-time and live big-time. As you follow me through these pages, you'll see that all the resources you need are already at your disposal. I've been studying this my entire life, I know this to be true, and I'm ready now to share what I've discovered with you.

A life in search of story

My background is in cognitive neuroscience and anthropology, so studying human behavior is a regular gig for me. I've studied chimpanzees and preliterate tribes and investigated how they use tools and rituals to affect their world. I've done extensive worldwide research on us modern humans and how we access the conceptual resources at our disposal to define and redefine ourselves. I'm endlessly fascinated by the ways in which people use what's in and around them to hold tight to—and sometimes expand—their own brand of meaning. I've been watching people create their stories for decades, and both the effort and the results are instructive.

We all have some natural abilities and some incapacities. I can easily attest to the latter myself. In spite of my fascination with the world's cultures and peoples, I cannot learn a foreign language, no matter how hard I try or how much time I devote to it. However, I've always had a natural interest and a modicum of ability to observe and assess the true nature of people. I remember at the age of seven telling my mother that I thought her friends, a married couple I observed at a dinner party at our house, would soon get a divorce (this was in the fifties, when divorce was less common and young children knew little about it). I felt this way about them despite the fact that I could not even hear them speak to each other because they were across the room. Later that night my mother scolded me for being presumptuous and brash. Some months after that, though, she told me that the couple was splitting up.

A while later, when I had just begun graduate school, I went to a presentation by two behavioral scientists describing their assessment of the relations between the guests they had analyzed from the home movies made at one son's birthday party. After that presentation I was manic for two days. These men were doing for a living what I thought I had it in me to do.

I went to one of them, Dr. Albert Scheflen, and after weeks of begging, I became one of his research assistants. That led to some breakthrough experiences for me. One thing his Project on Human Communication, at the Albert Einstein College of Medicine, did was get permission from a number of New York City families to place cameras in their homes to film them in situ. I watched many of those films, often more than once. Real life, not being cinematically directed, is of course slow and messy. But for me what was so fascinating and captivating was that you could see in real time almost all human qualities and frailties: the daily routines and the power of love, the courage and the weakness, the hesitancy and the passion, the coalitions and the individuality, the expected events and the unpredictable ones. Watching those films, I not only heard the stories; I *saw* the stories. And I was transfixed by it all.

Studying human nature and the nature of the mind—how it creates beliefs and attachments—was a natural for me. I craved

an understanding of people who lived by narrative and ritual, unencumbered by the accoutrements of modern, high-tech life. I
wanted, *needed* to see and experience life lived under a minimum
of outside influence. I felt this need because I am curious about
human behavior. But I am also selfish. In attempting to understand others, I understand my life better. One of the reasons you
will encounter so many stories in this book is that I believe the
stories of others always teach us something about ourselves.

The universal message of high achievement

In the course of my studies, I've become especially fascinated
with people who are following pursuits that fulfill them and feel
natural to them. Two projects of mine were particularly defining
here. One was studying people who were acknowledged as experts; the other was a study of small business owners. What has
become clear to me is that people living truly fulfilled lives have
something in common: They have the capacity to access, either
consciously or unconsciously, a deeper well of internal resources
than others do. They are using tools that most people don't use.
And for the most part they are having fun and are happy.

However, while their use of these resources is unique, the
resources themselves are not unique to them in any way. *These
resources exist for all of us.* They're part of our makeup as human
beings, and each of us has as much of a chance of using them effectively as anyone else has.

It's natural to look at others who have made great achievements
and think of them as outliers. The accomplished humanitarian,

scientist, athlete, artisan, and so on must be built differently than the rest of us. How else could they achieve what they've achieved?

Certainly, there's no arguing that some people have innate talents the rest of us simply don't have. If I tried to leap like Michael Jordan, my feet would barely leave the ground, and I'd probably wind up in traction. However, in terms of constituent capabilities, none of us are any different from Jordan or anyone else who has accomplished a great deal. In our own lives and on our own scale, we can embody the same processes as the most successful and acclaimed among us. You will discover stories in this book about people who have achieved tremendous fame, such as Richard Feynman, Jane Goodall, Wynton Marsalis, and Stella McCartney. These people all possess traits and behaviors that you will easily recognize, perhaps even in yourself.

Consider the case of Chuck Jones, the legendary animator who created the Road Runner and Pepé Le Pew, among many other characters who have tickled our imaginations for decades. Jones had several things working against him on his path to success, including a complicated, sometimes brutal childhood. However, he turned an early injury into a fundamental aspect of his personal story by giving credit to his fall off a roof for making him, as he put it, "not logical." Jones had a tremendous fascination with animals. He liked to draw, and would take any job that allowed him to do so. There's nothing particularly unusual about being interested in animals or enjoying drawing. These are traits that I would guess many readers of this book share. However, as you will discover in detail a few chapters down the road, Jones turned these interests into a tremendously successful career by applying a set of internal resources to them and doing something remarkable as a result, and he wound up living a life that was true to who he was. By using his innate capacity in a maximal way, Chuck Jones lived big. What he did was who he was. His was one of those stories that take on literary dimensions.

Making your story smaller than it needs to be

Maybe you're already living a life like the one Chuck Jones led. If so, congratulations. Maybe you can give your copy of this book to someone more needy. If not, you are hardly alone. In many if not most cases, the concept people have of their lives and how to live them—the stories they perceive about themselves—is too small. Many of us too soon succumb to external demands and internal "shoulds." Economics, tradition, lack of energy, and time constraints all come into play here. And we all know how easy it is to fall into a routine that is less than satisfying.

I understand "small" personally, from multiple perspectives. I came into the world way too small. I was a premature newborn weighing in at about one kilo (I like to say "one kilo"; it sounds better than 2.2 pounds), and I was in a precarious position. In order to survive, I had to stay in the hospital, living in an incubator-like box for more than forty days and forty nights. I see this time in the incubator as something of a metaphor for how most of us deal with the opportunities available to us: We can see them, but we feel incapable of leaving our boxes to pursue them.

I also understand the "small world" from a more symbolic perspective. I came from a loving family, but most everyone in it seemed to have a too-restricted point of view. My father died when I was very young, and this amplified my mother's fundamental hesitancy about life. She was vitally independent and a tough lady even in her elderly years, but her attitude toward the world is probably best captured by her oft-repeated phrase, "Don't go into the ocean because you might drown."

My father, on the other hand, was a dreamer. His untimely death served as a counterweight to my mother's cautiousness. After mourning his loss, I resolved to try to live life to the fullest, to make the most of whatever time I might have. To me this meant understanding who I truly am and how I fit into—and don't fit into—the world around me.

Meanwhile, I was conscious at a very early age that others in my family didn't really like what they did for a living, even though some of them were quite successful. They were good at their jobs; they just didn't find joy in them. I rejected this instinctively. I was interested in feeling alive—thriving, not just surviving. My response to my familiar surroundings was to become a kind of explorer, and I benefited from having two aunts, Pearl and Molly, who encouraged my exploratory nature. In some ways, my father's death liberated me, because it gave me an unusual level of freedom, since my mother had to go back to work. I used this freedom to learn as much about the world as I could. Even when I was very young, I spent a huge amount of time reading the encyclopedia, because I wanted to gather endless amounts of knowledge. This set me on a path to becoming a cognitive anthropologist, and to the observations that led to this book.

During my professional consulting practice in strategic marketing, I have been involved in projects for many corporations

and agencies worldwide. I have seen people who are working in
many different kinds of companies in various industries. Too
many times along the way, employees have come to me, an out-
sider they trust, bemoaning their busy workdays that leave little
room for them to express their own thoughts and points of view,
their true inner being. A recent such circumstance was one factor that compelled me to start writing this book. I was consulting for the Office of Strategy Development of a high-powered
company headquartered in Europe. As I was walking to lunch
one day with the head of this office, she asked me a question un-
related to my current engagement.

"Bob, we have just completed an internal survey by the HR
department on job satisfaction in our workforce. The results are
startling: high engagement and involvement, but low satisfaction. Could you explain this to me?"

I could have, but it would have taken a book to do so. For
now, let's just say that I wasn't surprised to hear this. In fact,
given how long I've been observing the workplace, I would have
been surprised to hear anything else. The simple fact is that most
people are like these employees and the people in my family.
They're competent, maybe even financially successful (maybe
even *very* successful financially), but they set the bar much too
low in their lives with respect to expressing their true essence—
to leading lives worthy of the great literary figures. There's a clear
reason for this. Fortunately, there's also a clear solution.

Tapping your essential resources

What my studies and observations have taught me is that we believe our capacities are limited because we don't realize that we have access to a remarkable set of resources that are as easy to use as they are profound in their ability to enhance the way we live. Once you start getting these resources to work for you, you begin to erect the story for yourself that you were meant to have.

I call these tools Essentials, because they are resident in all of us, because they are central to our being, and because they go a long way toward providing us clues to who we really are—to our essences. There are five of them, but I want to talk first about four:

- **CURIOSITY.** Curious people simply get more out of life because they make the effort to "look under the hood" and discover how the world operates. It is remarkable what you can uncover about any pursuit, passion, or even passing interest if you're curious about it. It is equally remarkable, though, that most people engage in the world with a minimum of curiosity. Choosing not to be curious is a bit like choosing not to pick up a hundred-dollar bill that you find on the sidewalk— except in this case, the sidewalk is littered with hundred-dollar bills. Myriad opportunities await anyone who uses the Essential of curiosity, paramount among which is the opportunity to discover something you never anticipated, and to have this become a fundamental part of the life you lead.

- **OPENNESS.** One of the greatest ways to live a richer life is to go into any pursuit unburdened by the need to know the ending at the beginning. I regularly consult with people at corporations who claim they are interested in learning more about consumer behavior. However, many of my clients try to skew the nature of the engagement to confirm a predetermined vision of the market. It sometimes takes the full use of my negotiating skills to get them to approach the project with openness. That's where all the magic is, though. When you set about your goals with an air of openness, you have an outcome in mind, but you are willing to embrace a different and better outcome. I call this phenomenon "directed serendipity." You allow the possibility of the extraordinary happening because you eschew preconceived notions of the result. When you employ this Essential, the rewards can be dizzying.

• **SENSUALITY.** I define sensuality as feeling your own experience of your own experience. In other words, it's about allowing yourself to make full use of your senses as you go through your life. As with the active employment of all Essentials, there's a certain amount of risk involved. Feeling more means that you will inevitably feel more unpleasantness. Understandably, there's strong motivation to avoid this. After all, while most of us feel less fulfilled than we'd like, few of us are in a constant state of misery. Why, then, take the chance of experiencing misery when you can skate across the top of your life instead, even if you're skating joylessly? The answer is that when you allow all of your senses to come online, when you dive deep into your life rather than skimming the surface, you let yourself interact with the world at the richest possible level.

- **PARADOX.** The world is never one thing or another, yet far too often we compartmentalize our experiences and our roles in just such a way. Something extraordinary happens when you start playing with ambiguities and contradictions, though: You start to see possibilities you never could have imagined. It's within those possibilities that most of us discover our most rewarding, meaningful, and authentic enterprises. What you will discover here is that *and* is one of the most liberating words in our language.

Each of these four Essentials works in the service of a fifth inner resource. This is the queen of all Essentials, the thing that allows you to fully believe that Jane Eyre and Sam-I-am have nothing on you.

Authoring your self-story

Self-story is the one thing a person needs—more than money, background, or IQ—to live a life of fulfillment, excitement, and personal innovation . . . to be happy.

We're going to get into this in depth later, but let's talk about self-story at a top-line level now. Self-story is the recurrent pattern of your being. It is the force driving your authentic self—all of it: its beauty and its warts, its brightness and its darkness. Self-story isn't your ideal or your hoped-for self. And your self-story is definitely not an autobiography or a chronological list of your life events. Self-story is the underlying design of *you as an idea* that stands above the press of the moment. It is, very simply put, what you are about. It is the you that exists beyond the day-to-day. It is the you that is consistently you, even though it is also evolving. You alone are the author of your self-story, and you alone have the power to change it, and if you are truly conscious of it—and this book will offer you a number of processes to help you gain that consciousness—then you can employ it to live the truest and most fulfilling version of the life you should be leading.

We'll go into the hows and whys of self-story later in the book. For now, let's just say that understanding your self-story is a hugely powerful resource. It helps you better understand where you're going. It allows you to decide what fits and doesn't fit in your life. And it allows you to make choices about your future in the context of the story you're already living, therefore allowing you to make changes that will genuinely improve your life and help you to accomplish what you truly want to accomplish.

Aspects of one's self-story are not all sunny or glamorous. I think the task we each have is at least to manage our darker side or, better yet, to shape a negative tendency into one that can be deployed in a productive way. My own self-story has aspects of fear and cynicism. As a result, there are times in my life when I have been gruff, short tempered, or negative. But I have also learned to put my fear to good use. To a great extent, my fear stems from the early loss I experienced when my father died. Even though I had my mother and a loving extended family, I felt abandoned and alone. So I overcompensated by trying to convince myself that my father's death didn't matter, that I would just do everything for myself. Out of this erroneous point of view, though, I eventually developed a healthy sense of personal responsibility. My father's death also left me quite the cynic. But people can change; they can evolve their self-stories. The birth of my daughter, a healthy child and an innately joyful human being who assumes that all interactions will be positive, changed me instantly and utterly, even though I was in my late thirties when she was born.

In my life, I have been very lucky to see many places on this planet of ours, from backwaters to luxury beaches, from rain forests to concrete jungles. I have met and studied heads of state, generals, farmers, scientists, grocery store clerks, business owners and employees, modern-day hip-hop stars, and tribespeople.

If there is one thing I have learned from the whole of my life and career, it is that the greatest joy comes from making your life into a search narrative, a search for the inward thing that you are and are becoming, a search for your own depths, excavating the unfathomable aspects—both beautiful and not so beautiful—of your true being.

Happily, in this search for one's self-story, there are no have-nots. All people, by virtue of being human beings, having experiences, and having the four other Essentials, can author self-stories that will anchor them and set them free to expand. The key is gaining vivid awareness of your developing self-story, because if you have that—if you truly know what you are about—a world of possibility emerges for you.

Today is a very good day to start

These five Essentials are the ones—and the only ones—that in the whole of my career and life experience I have found to consistently emerge across widely varying contexts of person and place. They therefore seem virtually universal. In the coming chapters I will explain each Essential in detail and personify them with interviews I did with women and men, some famous and some unknown, some younger, some older.

There couldn't be a better time than now to begin using your Essentials and especially to uncover your self-story. In addition to the general fact that many people live a life smaller than is necessary and therefore sell themselves and the world short, globalization and automation have produced a dangerously high unemployment rate, shaky economies, and unprecedented levels of uncertainty and change. A large number of people are now feeling painfully vulnerable and disenfranchised.

Likewise, corporate fear in a downturned economy has caused two opposite reactions: (1) many companies have become ever more hunkered down in their daily routines, and that has put human expressiveness on the firing line; and (2) other, more creative companies are thriving in this fast-changing world by hiring only people who can add value and constantly innovate. In the former case, thousands of people will seek career retraining or repositioning. In the latter case, creativity will be the primary talent necessary for upward mobility. Either way, satisfaction will come from *personal innovation*. To be innovative, people will need access to their own authenticity—and your Essentials, in the service of helping you create your self-story, will help make this possible.

Innovation, I have found, does not come from what you know. Innovation comes from passing what you know through the sieve of who you are. So you had better know who *you* are. The inner resources you will learn to master in this book will help you figure that out.

The primary way we gain insight into who we are is by using our other Essentials to feed our developing self-story. When we use our Essentials, we come face-to-face (occasionally many times in one day) with the recurrent themes in our lives and our overreactions. These seemingly fleeting moments contain clues to who we are and what we can do with who we are. If you aren't aware of your self-story, you can easily let these opportunities for growth pass you by. If you *are* aware, though, profound things can happen.

For example, when I was in my early twenties I saw the documentary film *Ladies and Gentlemen: The Rolling Stones.* When the film ended, I remained in my seat for a minute, overwhelmed. Without consciously knowing it, I had always been seeking the kind of energy and vigor that Mick Jagger exuded onstage. I walked out of the Ziegfeld Theatre on Fifty-fourth Street in Manhattan totally juiced. I was a just-uncaged animal. My reaction—my overreaction—was telling me something. I listened. That state of high arousal that comes from *doing who you are* was the feeling I wanted to live in. I always have that Ziegfeld moment at least in my peripheral vision.

Similarly, more than two decades later, I read a verbatim rendering in the *New York Times* of the speech Vaclav Havel, the then newly elected president of Czechoslovakia, gave to a joint session of the U.S. Congress. He was comparing explanation and understanding, saying that what the world needed most after the fall of the Soviet Union was understanding. Explanation, Havel said, saw the world's problems as resolvable through an objective procedure of successive approximations. Understanding, in sharp contrast, called for a more subjective stance, looking at life as lived in its enfolding, seeing life from the inside out. I have this speech framed and hanging on my office wall, and I read it often. It reminds me how much politics and business are devoid of the human scale. In politics and business there's little respect for and recognition of life as lived by everyday people. I fight constantly to make sure human understanding is injected in the veins of each businessperson in each business meeting I attend. It does no one any good to skim over the top of experience. You have to get into the guts of experience to understand yourself and life around you.

This respect and identification I have with everyday people—all people—is somewhat of a surprise to me. When I started my consulting practice in strategic marketing twenty-two years ago, I thought it would be fun and that I could make some money at it. I wanted to live the high life, a life now recalled in the award-winning TV show *Mad Men*.

What I found, though, was not what I had intended. I found out something fundamental about my self-story and me. I was not a mercenary. I was a person with a deep sense of what a life is and a feeling for the common good. I still had my various forms of selfishness, but for the most part they revolved around just wanting to feel and wanting to understand me, understand others, and understand me through my reactions to others.

As part of my work I spend a good deal of time talking with people in what are commonly called focus groups. These group participants, overall, have come from every walk of life. My groups are unique. In them I don't ask people about any particular product or service. I ask them something like, "How's life?" or "What's life like for you nowadays?" I have the naive belief that if you truly understand some things about people's lives, you can design ways to uplift those lives, and as a result uplift sales. I like to tell the marketing audiences I give speeches to that if you want to be a great marketer, you need to forget about marketing and think about life. Then you'll be a great marketer.

In the process of doing my group discussions (I call them "thinkering groups" because I'm interested in understanding how the mind tinkers with thoughts to create meaning), I have uncovered something about me that in the most profound way is why I do my work the way I do it and why I wrote this book. My gift, the one thing I'm innately good at, is helping people bring forth their own story. My groups are long (usually close to three hours) and some say grueling. I don't let people off the hook. I challenge them to go beyond stereotypical or clichéd talk. I point out what I hear as contradictions in what they are now saying in the group compared with what they said an hour ago. I want to help people to get under the cover story of their business as usual. That's where the revealing moments and the valuable surprises are. I have no preplanned questions (other than the one I open with), and I make it known that top-of-mind answers are insufficient. I'm not sure what's going to happen at any given moment in the group, nor are the participants. But that's life—a complex mix of irony, humor, and drama.

What I'm trying to do in these groups is get people to live at the level of *the self as an idea*. I'm trying to get them to understand what they are about—what motivates them at the deepest possible level, what their big themes are, and where their lives are taking them overall, not just today or tomorrow. My hope is that they will understand the life stories they are authoring (often unconsciously, at least until they meet me) for themselves, embrace those stories, and understand the control they have over those stories. I get to this by raising many of the issues and asking many of the questions that you're going to read in this book. The goal of all of this is twofold: to make people aware that they have this Essential of self-story at their disposal, and to help them to see that mastering it gives them tremendous power over their futures.

The beautiful thing is, although most people are not accustomed to experiencing themselves this way, when I create the context for them to do it, most find they are comfortable with and capable of the experience. Amazingly, when I feel the arc of the session is spent and I end the group, people often don't want to leave. After all, they came with the expectation that they were going to get a few bucks and a sandwich; in my sessions they tend to come away with much more than that.

Sometimes my business clients watch these sessions in a room with a one-way mirror with the permission of the group participants. It is not uncommon for these clients to ask me after a group ends, "Dr. Bob, can you do that with me?" Once you begin the journey to uncovering your self-story, it's addictive, because it feels so right and so freeing. You feel your energy becoming unblocked. You feel yourself moving toward your destiny.

Looking back, I've always been an extractor of stories and a storyteller. My mother says that my kindergarten teacher told her that I was an interesting child. Why? Because I got along with every different type of child. The teacher told my mother why this was so: I listened and showed that I listened.

My paternal grandparents, Abe and Eva, were storytellers, at least to me. I would often sit on my grandfather's knee with a bowl of nuts in my lap that he would crack open as he began embellishing one of his favorite opera librettos or folktales. My grandmother was the greatest cook in the world. She had a very wide windowsill, like an alcove, in her kitchen, which I would sit on while she cooked and told me stories of the history of certain recipes she was making and the people and situations she associated with, say, her sweet and sour pot roast. My mouth waters even as I write these words, and my mind is set reeling from all the feelings those kitchen memories evoke in me.

Likewise, when I was a teenager, many of my friends and even some older acquaintances would come to me about a situation or problem or decision that was on their mind and ask, "What do you think?" I very rarely gave advice, but I did get these people to consider things on their own.

Uncovering that as a major part of my self-story has allowed me to make a career of that inclination. This gives me great satisfaction, joy, and energy. That is the promise of this book. You too, in authoring your self-story with the help of the four other Essentials, will better know the true you, and you will also gain a firmer footing in the world as you forever explore and evolve *you*.

In the process of authoring your self-story, you will find fulfillment and success, and you will become more innovative with your own life. But it will be all those things as *you* define them and as *you* experience them. As your self-story evolves, your goals might change, or how you think about what you intend can change. There are no rules or predefined procedures. It's up to you and what you feel, how you respond to things you sense and are open to, and how trusting of yourself you are.

How this book works

This book is divided into two parts. The first part lays out each of the five Essentials, defining them and showing you why these resources are so fundamental to your life. The back end of the book then walks you through five processes that combine the Essentials in important ways, allowing you to master the creation of your self-story.

- **ALWAYS BE ON YOUR WAY HOME.** One of the keys to living a life of fulfillment is to have a clear sense of your destination *without ever reaching your destination.* This might sound contradictory, but mastering this process is revelatory.

- **OWN YOUR NARRATIVE.** There's a difference between being aware of your self-story and taking true ownership of it. When you do the latter, your self-story works for you at all times.

- **STOP AND FOCUS.** Taking a moment to gather yourself might seem like a luxury given the pace at which we all seem to be living. However, once you come to understand this process, you'll realize that it is a luxury you absolutely must afford yourself.

- **RIFF ON THE WORLD.** We admire the virtuosos in the world because of their ability to create something distinctive within the structure of their disciplines. For example, a great jazz soloist riffs on a musical chart to bring something fresh and exciting to a piece. All of us are capable of similar virtuosity within our chosen disciplines.

- **VITALIZE.** One of the most energizing and exciting aspects of living the truest version of your life is that doing so has the potential to bring increased vitality to the lives of others. When you consciously attempt to vitalize, what you often find is that you feel a greater sense of vitality yourself.

As is only appropriate in a book of this type, most of what you will discover in these pages comes in the form of example rather than dictate. Instead of telling you exactly how to employ these resources and how to author your self-story, I'm going to offer you examples that I believe are especially instructive. There are lots and lots of stories in this book. I think you'll find them both entertaining and illuminating.

In the end, my goal in writing this book is to help you understand that you can expect much more from your life than you might believe right now. You have a right to an ongoing series of fulfilling experiences, and you have every reason to pursue them—especially when you yourself might be your biggest impediment to living such a life, and you yourself have everything inside you to live it. This is particularly true if you avoid preconceived notions of what fulfillment means and choose instead to accept fulfillment however it comes to you. This isn't necessarily about winning championships or grabbing the corner office. You don't need to conquer the world in order to feel like you're sitting on top of it. You just need to do who you are.

And even more than expecting authenticity and fulfillment, what you should absolutely expect is that your life should bring you fun. This is maybe the most consistent trait among people who are truly employing their Essentials: They seem to be having more fun than everyone else. Have you ever noticed how the energy level changes when someone who has a real sense of self and mission enters the room? The air seems to get lighter, the day sunnier. That's because these people are having fun. They are enjoying being alive, and they are giving us a glimpse of this with their presence. The fact is, though, that you don't need others to make you feel this way. You just need the full employment of your Essentials.

The day I discovered this powerful suite of resources resident in every person was one of the brightest days of my life. That day, I realized that the fulfillment of potential and the blueprint for living authentically doesn't require an abundance of good fortune. Nor does it need to be directed by others. It requires only awareness of the essentials and the understanding of some basic processes.

This is what I am offering you here. You can live a life worthy of a literary classic. There is a great story inside you.

Let's start to get it out.

part 1

YOUR INNER RESOURCES

chapter one

The Essential of Curiosity

B Y ANYONE'S DEFINITION, Michael Spiessbach is someone who has put himself out into the world. He was admitted to the bar in 1972, he has been a corporate attorney, he is at home in the middle of multibillion-dollar deals, and he has served as president of a major television production company. He is an authority on international business, and he negotiated the world's first investment in something not physically on earth (Canada's Anik C1 satellite). He has been involved in business ventures in more than seventy countries, and he has strong interests in areas ranging from cosmology to comparative religion to martial arts. So much fascinates him, and this makes him a singularly fascinating person.

"As you go through life," he told me, "you bump into things and they bump into you. You take the measure of them from an evolutionary point of view—are you dangerous to me? Are you helpful to me? What you run into from a brute encounter perspective is limited because you have to physically run into it. But there is an unlimited encounter if you open the door of curiosity and you look beyond what is just there and seek what's not there."

For Spiessbach, this approach to the world began to express itself when he was young.

"I don't know how old I was, maybe ten or twelve. I was reading in one of those orange-papered books, more like comic books, and it had different stories about things. One was about Carter discovering the tomb of Tutankhamen; another was about the Maori tribe in New Zealand. I remember being fascinated by these and having a feeling that I wanted to go there—*I want to go to the pyramids; I want to go to New Zealand*. It was a physical wanderlust beyond the confinement of my neighborhood, which was for many practical purposes my universe."

A professor in an art class that Spiessbach took as an undergrad ratcheted this up to the next level.

"I had to get rid of some humanities credits in college, and I had no inclination toward humanities at that point. Really, none toward art. This one student counselor I went to, he said, 'Are you interested in music?' I said, 'I like music, but I don't know anything about music.' 'Are you interested in art?' 'Yeah, visual, sounds easy.' He said, 'If you take art, only take Dr. Weber.' Those few words from someone I really didn't know profoundly and radically affected my entire life. It was by serendipity that I came to be in Dr. Weber's class. It was a realization that there's so much more than I had been aware of, led to believe that there was. I found exposure to that satisfying. I wanted to be exposed to as much as possible. In his case, it happened to be art, from Paleolithic art, to Indian art, to Chinese art, to Japanese art, to contemporary art. It was an entirely different way of broadening your mind, to see things very differently than I'd been raised and developed to see them.

"He showed a slide one day from the Altamira fresco. It was a very rough drawing of what we would say is a tic-tac-toe board, except it was twenty-five thousand years old. He asked everyone in the class what this was, and everyone answered from their own frame of reference. It's a tic-tac-toe board. No. It's a window with panes. No, that didn't exist at that point in time. It's a corral. No, animals hadn't been domesticated at that point in time. He dragged everyone through the process of removing your normal thoughts. His suggestion was that this was a representation of something that the artist had never seen or experienced in his physical life. It did not physically exist; therefore it was a physical representation of a nonphysical event, a thought. That suggested to me how to approach things. What is that you're looking at? What is that you're confronting? What is that you're experiencing? Don't be limited by your first instinctive reaction. Go beyond it; deconstruct it.

"An artist is willing—by my definition of an artist—to sacrifice everything to find his or her art, not even knowing what his or her art may ultimately be. It's a process of finding what is meaningful to you. It's the realization that there's more than what you know, and that you want to find that which is more than what you know. I think Einstein said curiosity is more important than knowledge, and I think that's what he was talking about. You search for that which you don't know you're searching for."

Over time, Spiessbach developed an approach to the world that allowed him to extend himself even further.

"When I turned fifty, I felt that I had enough time and

residence to be able to speak on things. What you should do until then is to mostly listen and experience. I decided to question everything in my life, to doubt everything, to go back to the very beginning of everything. That led me to a process, to a conclusion that I coined 'becoming a forensic realist.' I concluded, in looking back and questioning everything, that each of us is born into a default operating system. These default modes of thinking are done by institutional vested interest groups. They may be parental, they may be priestly, they may be political, they may be professorial, but they have an institutional bias against curiosity. Because what they believe that they have and what they're either instilling in you, with goodwill or not, is a sense of certainty, which means safety. Whenever you go beyond certainty into curiosity, you're taking a risk.

"To be a forensic realist, you have to be open to whatever the evidence leads to. I believe most people find comfort in not having to run that risk, because that risk may lead to something other than what they believe they were molded for from their childhood. You run a risk when you seek. There is a possibility that it could be very, very bad or a possibility that it could be very, very good. But the likelihood is that it's going to be somewhere in between or some mixture. But it probably will be not what you go into it with as an accepted premise.

"Woody Allen once said ninety-nine percent of success is showing up. You have to be out there. You have to be exposed. If you just sit and vegetate, nothing happens. It's not going to happen—you have to go out. You don't know what's going to happen, but that's part of the joy of it."

Perhaps more than anyone I've ever met, Michael Spiessbach

has mastered his Essential of curiosity. It has had an enormous influence on his self-story, it has served him remarkably well in his career, and it has given him perspectives that have allowed him to accomplish things that others could only approximate. More important, though, it has given him a tremendous sense of fulfillment and excitement about life and a richness of experience that we all should want to—and can—share.

> Ever tried? Ever failed? No matter. Try again. Fail again. Fail better.
>
> —Samuel Beckett

Behind the glowing door

Curiosity is the innate desire to seek out the new, to delight in the possibility of surprise that exists around every corner if you're open to finding it. When people engage their curiosity, they make a conscious move toward the unknown and delight in the experience.

The image that always comes to my mind when I think about curiosity is the scene very early in Steven Spielberg's *Close Encounters of the Third Kind*. A young boy is in his home when the brilliant light from a landing alien ship blazes through the cracks in the door frame of his house. The glowing door temporarily mesmerizes the boy . . . and then he steps toward it. I'm not sure that there's a better illustration out there of the idea of curiosity. Something is on the other side of the door. It might be friend or foe, providence or damnation—but you need to find out what it is.

What underpins curiosity is a love of learning. I'm not talking specifically about schooling here, though certainly one gets more from school if one is curious. What I'm talking about is the aliveness that comes from a perpetual desire to find out more. When you're curious, you interact with the world in a way that leads you to welcome new information, embrace challenges, and celebrate being moved out of your comfort zone. Curiosity compels you to discover something new, to dig deeper into something you already know, or to expose yourself to common experiences in uncommon ways.

There's interesting recent research that speaks to the value of interdisciplinary knowledge. One of the core tenets of interdisciplinarity is that throwing together experts from different domains allows perspectives that the experts would never consider when focusing exclusively on their own domain. When one has a problem to tackle in domain X, one gathers experts in X to attack it. However, if at the same time one adds a couple of non-X people to the group, the X people come up with more creative and productive solutions.

This is curiosity at work. The non-X people look at the problem from an entirely different perspective because they don't have the vocabulary of or a deep background in X. The observations they make are likely to be useless in regard to addressing the problem directly. However, by shining a different light on the problem, they activate the curiosity of those with the skills to develop a workable solution. The X people, armed with curiosity and a surprise perspective, can then overcome barriers to their thought processes.

I witnessed a version of this firsthand years ago when I did some work with the great trial attorney Edward Bennett Williams. Williams had hired me to offer my insight as an anthropologist on a few of his cases. Not long into our working relationship, I realized that the primary dynamic between us involved my presenting him with something and his yelling at me about what I'd presented. "Bob, I can't use this information," he would often say at high volume. "There are such things as rules of evidence in a courtroom." I realized he was right; my pedestrian knowledge of how courtrooms functioned was causing me to feed him details he could never introduce into his trials. Chastened, I asked him if he could provide me with the opportunity to audit a rules-of-evidence class at Georgetown, since he sat on the university's law school board.

I felt good about my sense of initiative for exactly one second before Williams said, "Bob, let me know when you start that course. I'll fire you that day because then you'll be useless to me. I can't use the things you say to me directly in court, but if what you say helps me just one time in one case by opening my thinking, that's why you're here."

Williams was one of the legendary figures in his field. One of the reasons he was so uncommonly effective at what he did was that he was curious enough to think of hiring an anthropologist simply because at some point I might accidentally say something valuable.

> We shape our tools, and thereafter our tools
> shape us.
>
> —Marshall McLuhan

Curious soul in the side pocket

There are two types of curiosity. Let's call them "active" and "passive." Active curiosity involves consciously seeking new and different experiences. Michael Spiessbach is an actively curious person because he's on an endless search for the new. His entire approach to what he calls "forensic realism" requires active engagement with the unknown. He's doing this because he knows that for him it's the most effective way to get closer to understanding how the world works.

Passive curiosity doesn't involve making a determined effort to discover. Instead, the passively curious person adopts an attitude that invites the *possibility* of discovery. My sense is that there are far more passively curious people in the world than actively curious ones, and I count myself among the former group. For a long time now, I have characterized myself as a billiard ball in the universe. I have a certain mass and velocity, and when set in motion I occasionally bump into something, and that changes the course of both the thing I bump into and myself. As a passively curious person, I'm not seeking anything in particular; I'm simply letting myself go where my insides say it's exciting. I've done some of my best work by taking this approach, I've expanded myself considerably in the process, and I can honestly say that because of this, I tend to enjoy what I'm doing most days.

It doesn't particularly matter if you use your innate sense of curiosity in an active or passive way, as this is largely a matter of temperament. What's important is that, however you use it, you *use it*. Curiosity is one of the five Essentials because you can't effectively understand what you are capable of and what you need to do to realize that capability if you aren't on a lifelong search. People who sequester themselves, who close themselves off to possibility, rarely accomplish anything truly significant. Really, how could they? By nature, if you lock yourself away from new experiences, how can you ever break ground? History doesn't celebrate those who maintain the status quo, and while cultures occasionally show an increased appetite for nostalgia, no culture thrives for long on a policy of moving backward.

In my experience, the truly fine practitioners in any domain— the Edward Bennett Williamses and Michael Spiessbachs of the world—are very curious people. Their very strongly developed sense of curiosity drives them to invent, reimagine, shift focus, and alter direction. By asking what if, why, and how, they see the world in ways that less curious people don't. As a result, they do things with the world that others never consider.

However, while these people might be very gifted, curiosity itself is not a gift. This is an important point to underscore here and for you to remember as you continue reading this book. I have never met anyone without at least some sense of curiosity, nor have I ever read a report or a paper about a syndrome that suppresses or eliminates it. Curiosity is inherent in all of us; it is always available and operating in the background, like the virus protection program on your computer. We all have curiosity built into us—when we ask a question, look around a corner, pursue something new (even something as mundane as ordering a never-before-tried menu item), or vacation somewhere different than before. If you don't consider yourself to be a curious person, there's a good chance that you've decided, either consciously or otherwise, not to be curious.

The couch potatoes of curiosity

Curiosity is a wondrous tool. When you are curious, you see the world as a place of endless possibility. The potential for surprise and delight exists around every corner—as does yet another opportunity to expand and enhance yourself.

Why, then, do so many people in the world shun curiosity? To be perfectly candid, one reason is laziness. Being curious requires more effort than accepting things as they are. It's so much easier to do things as you've always done them or to follow well-worn paths. Most people understand that their curiosity is likely to lead to new discoveries, but they also understand that those new discoveries will almost surely compel them to expend additional effort. Therefore, they relax with the tried and true. Choosing not to exercise your curiosity is much like choosing not to exercise your body: The cost is not immediately detrimental, and it's much less tiring in the short term.

I had a boss years ago, when I worked for the government, who was extremely smart. He understood things about policy, negotiation, and program management that I'm sure I'll never be able to understand, regardless of how curious I am. However, he was a shadow of what he might have been, because he took an extremely lazy and uncurious approach to his work. When he was faced with a problem, his instinctual response was to fit the solution into the box of what he'd done before. He had a handful of approaches to challenges, and he showed no interest in exploring new approaches. This had nothing to do with mental capacity; the man was exceedingly bright. He simply couldn't be bothered, and the result was that he accomplished so much less with his life than he should have.

However, even highly motivated people can succumb to the seduction of sticking with the familiar. That's because familiarity is one of the key components of the human experience. We can't live in the new constantly—if we did, we wouldn't have time to be curious, because we'd be spending all of our time just trying to figure things out. I consider myself extremely curious, but when I get out of bed in the morning, I prefer to walk to the bathroom the same way I did the day before, brush my teeth in the same manner, and drink my coffee in the same chair. I don't choose on some days to get out of bed on the left side, on the right on others, and out the foot of the bed on yet others. I don't have any interest in eating breakfast in the dining room one day, the kitchen the next, and the driveway the day after that. The familiarity of these little rituals is comforting to me, and that comfort is an important part of my emotional makeup. The human central nervous system is an inherently conservative operation. It couldn't possibly handle one hundred percent new information all the time.

Familiarity, therefore, is fundamental. Familiarity feels good. We like old friends, old sweaters, and old habits. There are many foods we like to eat often, songs we like to hear regularly, and stories we like to repeat and have repeated to us. It's not surprising that people get caught up in familiarity and keep their curiosity at bay. As my old boss would tell you, there's a strong sense of security in doing things the way you've always done them.

As long as you don't have any interest in growing, in becoming that unforgettable literary character we discussed earlier. If you *are* interested in growing, though, then you need to engage your curiosity as often as your brain will allow. Exploration keeps us alive. Consider the very simple fact that if we'd maintained the status quo as a species, we would be long extinct because we would have failed to adapt to the environment as it changed around us. Equally important, novelty seeking allows you to have a sense of being connected to things outside of yourself and bigger than yourself, and it allows you to play a meaningful role in the changes happening around you.

The necessity of "next"

One of the reasons that curiosity is so valuable in aiding self-expansion is that one of the core questions curiosity prompts is, "What's next?" This is one of the key considerations for anyone hoping to build on one's life, as it naturally leads you to put your life in context. You can't accurately identify what you should do next if you don't know what you've already done. This, by extension, leads you to consider who you are and who you want to be, an essential step in embracing your self-story.

Curiosity is all about "next." What do I do *next*? Where do I go *next*? What's *next* on my agenda? When you regularly pose these questions to yourself, you tend to feel more alive because your life seems to have momentum. "Next" implies action and progress. If you're thinking about what's next, you tend to have a powerful sense that your life is moving in a forward direction.

I strongly believe that this is universal, regardless of culture. It is, in fact, a fundamental indicator of cultural vibrancy. When we think of the cultures surging onto the world stage—India and South Korea, for example—we see they have a very strong sense of next. They're rushing headlong into tomorrow, creating, innovating, and evolving. Conversely, when we think of cultures in decline or locked in hopelessness—large chunks of central Asia and North Korea, for instance—we think of places that have no workable way of dealing with next.

One would think of China as a hotbed of next, and in many ways this is true. I've recently done a great deal of work in Beijing, and I've come away with the realization that while a culture can have a burgeoning sense of curiosity about the future, different segments within that culture can have wildly different angles on this.

While I was in Beijing, I conducted a series of interviews focusing on perspectives about the present and the future. The responses broke strongly along generational lines. People between fifty-five and sixty-five, those who came of age during the Cultural Revolution and have seen their country go through overwhelming political change in the past six decades, tend to see the future philosophically. People in this group regularly told me that while they'd had many hard times living under Mao, there had been a clarity about the future that came from living under one idea—even if that idea was exclusively Mao's. Now they see the future as a jumble of the optimistic and the pessimistic, of progress and disruption. Having seen so much change in their lives, they tend to be cautious about "next," and they consistently said to me that they were looking for some small positive thing to latch onto.

Thirty-five- to forty-five-year-olds could not be more different. This group isn't old enough to remember the Cultural Revolution, and they've spent about half of their lives in China's unique mix of communism and capitalism. This group consistently talked about the future as an opportunity to acquire more things. They have more money than they've ever had and they even have more time to spend it than they did before, and they're looking for as many goodies as they can buy, feeling that having more things will lead to increased status.

The most surprising answers I received to questions about the future came from the youngest group I interviewed, nineteen to twenty-five. These people have lived their entire lives in an open China. They learned in school about Mao and about China's millennia of tradition, but the only world they've experienced is one of constant flux, a world in which change happens daily. Interestingly, growing up in an all-next-all-the-time world has led them to idealize the past. They regularly told me that they felt cheated by not having the old rituals, teachings, and traditions. They didn't want the life of endless competition that they faced. They longed for simplicity. Of course, the historical China they spoke of during these conversations never existed, and they ignored the distressingly hard lives most people lived back then, but it was instructive to me to see how people react when "next" becomes the overwhelming cultural driver.

Still, regardless of where any of these groups stood, they had incorporated "next" into their lives in a holistic way. There are very few people in industrialized China who shun the future. They might not always embrace what that future holds, but they tend to understand that they need to take an interest in where their lives are going.

To me, this illustrates why curiosity is so critical to our evolution as individuals. We might not always like what's in the offing, but when we contribute to what comes next we live more engaged lives, and we stand a far better chance of feeling good about the outcome of our lives.

> We are stardust in the highest exalted way.
>
> —Neil deGrasse Tyson

Toying with genius

Often curiosity leads to breakthroughs that you would never otherwise encounter. Other times, it simply serves to energize you and nourish you in incalculable ways. I had one such experience many years ago, with the Nobel Prize–winning physicist Richard Feynman. Because they wanted to find a way to train better political analysts, the U.S. government hired me to create a new definition of *expertise*. One of the primary ways in which I chose to approach the work was by interviewing and observing a dozen people from different areas of expertise, one of whom was Feynman.

Feynman was known for his outsize personality and his joie de vivre, and both were on ample display from the moment we met. He asked me about myself, and I gave him a brief summary of my background, mentioning that I had majored in math as an undergrad. This got us around to talking about various mathematical conundrums.

Feynman paused for a moment and then said, "Well, you know, there have been advances in some of those realms." And then his eyes brightened. "But let's you and me spend some time on one of those as if it's the first time we heard about it."

To me, this exchange distills the absolute pleasure of curiosity. Feynman could have recommended that I look up the papers that had already been published on the topic. Instead, he suggested that we look at this problem as if there was not already a solution in the works and as if we'd just come up with the idea, just so we could live through some of the excitement of parsing it out ourselves. What Feynman understood, and what all of us can experience in our own domains, is that the exercise of applying your curiosity to a problem can reap benefits much greater than simply eliminating the problem. I not only came away from that day in Feynman's presence with an unforgettable memory, but my mind felt energized by the interaction. We didn't get very far in our work, and it would have been a poor use of a great man's time for me to suggest that we continue to pursue it together, but I saw the world a little differently afterward.

The playground of curiosity

Recently, I was hired by the discount retailer TJX to study the behavior of the customers and noncustomers of their Marshalls and HomeGoods stores. As a consumer, I was decidedly in the noncustomer category when it came to these establishments. When I walked into one of these stores, all I saw was clutter—racks and shelves filled with disparate merchandise with little or nothing to help me make a selection. TJX has built an extremely successful retail model around offering deep discounts in a bare-bones setting, but when I went into the engagement, I wrongly assumed that their customers were people who wanted nice things but couldn't afford to buy them in more refined shopping environments.

As I started interviewing these customers, though, I realized that I'd completely missed the point—Marshalls and HomeGoods stores are a prime attraction for the curious. "You'll always find something that you don't even know you're looking for" was a common comment. "There's always a great deal; there's always a great item. There just always is. You're never disappointed." These customers saw themselves as explorers, digging through the varied racks with the expectation that a treasure was waiting for them. While the value pricing was important to them, what was considerably more important was the sense of adventure. They consistently told me that shopping at these stores made life seem less mundane and that it provided an extended high.

"I like to be spontaneously drawn to something," one shopper said, going on to tell me about how the store engaged her imagination. She could find a blouse among the mix and immediately envision wearing it. She could find a vase on a shelf and instantly get the image of it on her coffee table. "My eyes can see it," she told me. "It stands out. It's different. It's me."

TJX shoppers spoke about their experiences with a level of delight uncommon among retail customers I've interviewed over the years. What they were really doing, though, was singing the praises of curiosity. These customers—very definitely in the actively curious camp—found enormous and ongoing rewards in allowing themselves to find out what was behind the glowing door. Their time in these stores was thrilling, surprising, and fulfilling. They didn't always find something to buy, but when they did, they felt a strong sense of accomplishment. They felt victorious.

This is a testament to the rewards of curiosity. Much of life is like those racks at Marshalls: It's cluttered, it's cacophonous, and there are very few signs to guide us. However, for the curious, for those who are willing to explore life's offerings with a sense of adventure and excitement, the possibility of finding something wonderful is considerable.

chapter two

The Essential of Openness

A FEW YEARS BACK, I did an extensive study of small business owners for American Express. While I try to enter every engagement with as few preconceived notions as I can, I'd heard plenty of opinions over the years about why people want to run their own operations. The terms that I heard most commonly were *control*, *freedom*, and *peace of mind*. However, I was no further than a third of the way into this study when I realized that these terms had little relation to what small business owners really wanted.

Being in control wasn't anywhere near the top of the priority list. In fact, what seemed to excite the majority of the people I interviewed was the idea that their lives were subject to a constant stream of surprise and change in direction. They understood that trying to control things too carefully was counterproductive, since all of their big leaps in productivity and success came because of something they couldn't have designed or anticipated.

They did value freedom, especially those who came from

restrictive corporate backgrounds. However, the pleasure they derived from freedom came less from being free to do whatever they wanted and more from being free to sink or swim on their own merits without having someone make critical decisions for them. The freedom they sought was the freedom to react in the moment to the changes facing their enterprises without the encumbrances of a corporate hierarchy.

Most of them laughed when I mentioned peace of mind in the context of their work. The very notion that one should start a small business in search of peace was to them a complete contradiction. Peace, in fact, seemed to be the antithesis of what they sought. Most associated peace of mind with stasis, telling me that if you had peace of mind, it meant that you'd stalled out or that you'd "closed your doors." Several even equated it with death.

While the terms I brought to the engagement became less and less relevant in my mind with every interview, another word emerged as one that defined both the objectives and the ambitions of someone who chooses to pursue a career this way. It was a word that described both a necessary attribute and a trait that offered the most likely path to success.

That word was *open*.

The people I interviewed for this study spoke regularly about their desire to discover new things, to avoid boredom, and to grow in unexpected ways. They understood that to do so, they needed to allow themselves to face the future with a mind-set that allowed for a diversion from the plan. They needed to have a good idea of their business model, while acknowledging that this model couldn't possibly anticipate every eventuality or opportunity. Several of them even equated openness with using George

Lucas's Force—surrendering yourself to the flow in order to increase your powers.

"You sort of go down a path and things evolve," one interviewee said to me. "By adapting and adjusting to randomness, you shape but do not control your endpoint. But you define your endpoint by your own reaction to it: 'Aha! I like this. This is for me. This *is* me.'"

Small business owners are in many ways the people who do the most with their self-stories. Overwhelmingly, they equate their identities with their professions; their businesses reflect who they are. As one interviewee put so succinctly, "My company is me, and I hope I can be more of me." Therefore, success in their business equates with success in their selves, and this means that they will use whichever tools help them to grow their businesses, because that has deeply personal meaning for them. In addition, they rarely have safety nets and they rarely have backup, so it's critical that they adopt practices that reduce their chances of failure. It's instructive, then, to see that they put such a premium on openness.

"I'm daring to do what I imagined," another interviewee told me. "I'm fighting to be me. That means that when doors open, you sometimes walk in."

"Being out of my comfort zone is exciting," yet another said. "I love being out on the edge. Being on the edge is exciting and enchanting."

"Be open to what comes," said someone else, "and you can make it come."

Even how they discovered what they were meant to be doing required a high level of openness to possibility. Nearly everyone

I interviewed told me a story about a revelatory moment. That moment might have come very early in life (several people spoke of realizing what they wanted to do when they were still young children), during a crisis while they were working for someone else, or by what they described as sheer luck. In every case, these revelations happened because the person involved was open to the possibility of revelation; possibility itself was a welcome and wonderful thing.

What emerged most clearly for me from these sessions was that a majority of small business owners subscribe to, even if only at the subconscious level, what I've come to call an "open plan." They move forward in a particular direction, they leave themselves open to changing direction, they learn from their openness, and they arrive at a new yet ever-evolving place that is exponentially richer than where they started.

What better testament is there to the value and life-enhancing quality of this Essential? For the small business owners I studied, openness allowed them to discover professions that drive them and guide them. And, as we will discuss in the coming pages, the value of openness is hardly limited to professional accomplishment. Openness enhances every aspect of your life, provides you with countless new options, and allows for the happiest of surprises.

> Don't be afraid to be confused. Try to remain permanently confused. Anything is possible. Stay open forever, so open it hurts, and then open up some more.
>
> —George Saunders, *The Braindead Megaphone*

Increasing the chances of surprise and delight

People who live fulfilled lives tend to have a fundamental thing in common: They're open. This is not coincidental. Openness is critical to having a strong sense of fulfillment, because only if you are open can you truly experience your life. Only if you are open can you go beyond the surface of what you experience to get to the richness and nuance that lies underneath.

Not long ago, I was speaking with Anne, a corporate executive who told me that she'd recently started playing the cello. While Anne is starting this pursuit relatively late in life, she has always heard cello music in her head and has always aspired to make this music. When she was young, her sister was obsessed with extraterrestrials (this is someone who would most definitely go through the glowing door we mentioned earlier) and would talk about them all the time. Whenever Anne thought about the sounds that extraterrestrials might make, she heard a cello playing.

As much as she loved the instrument, the early steps of learning to play were challenging for her. Her hands are small, and she couldn't get around the cello as easily as someone with longer fingers would. Her early months of practice involved long hours of exercises to build up her finger muscles, and these exercises hardly generated beautiful music.

However, as she became more adept at playing, she noticed something profound. "You can move your finger on a string just an iota," she told me, "and it changes the tone." She became fascinated with how these little adjustments brought new levels of expressiveness to her playing and how she could incorporate this shading into her performance to bring levels of depth she could never achieve otherwise.

To me, this is a vivid illustration of what openness offers us. Life isn't about simply working as hard as you can to hit the right notes in a piece. It's about allowing yourself to hear the nuances associated with playing the note a little differently and, if you find a version that you really like, deciding to play the piece that way in the future. Where curiosity is about allowing your mind to be tickled and enhanced by exposure to something new, openness is about allowing the unanticipated to affect the course of your life. Anne never would have gotten as much from her playing if she hadn't been open to how little adjustments changed the sound. And while most of us will never play the cello, there's much we can take away from her experience.

Openness requires giving yourself the chance to *feel*, not simply react. When you're open, you allow the world to seep into you at a different level. This isn't possible if you're busy responding to every stimulus you face. Sometimes this means filing away an experience or an emotion for later use. Doing so allows you to enhance the quality of your reactions and your experiences; the deeper the pool you can draw on, the more varied your experience will be.

I see this—or, more accurately, the opposite—in business all the time. When I have client meetings, I'm astounded by how often people come to the meeting absolutely closed to possibility. People will sit around the table speaking from their established positions, and as a result they add nothing of value. It's the corporate equivalent of going on automatic pilot. One would imagine that you could accomplish as much by sending preprogrammed holograms into the meeting instead of real people. You wouldn't get anything more done, but you could save money on coffee and pastries.

This is often true even when a disruptive force, like me, is added to the mix. The marketing people are fully locked into how marketing operates within the company, the salespeople are fully locked into how sales operates within the company, the product development people are fully locked into how product development operates within the company, and so on. The culture is so closed and intransigent that a provocateur like me needs to struggle mightily to get anyone to consider another point of view—even when the people in the room know that I was hired to be a provocateur.

Every now and then, though, I run into someone willing to consider the possibility that his or her company hasn't predetermined every eventuality, and that it might be productive to look at things in new ways. This person tends to be very high up in the company or on a fast track within the company. Again, this isn't a coincidence. These people are succeeding in a world of hardline positions because they understand that being open to possibility doesn't negate everything you've done before (though it might); instead it enhances it.

This of course applies far beyond the business world. Openness makes all kinds of experiences richer, whether they are interpersonal relationships, hobbies, family dynamics, or even vacations. Perhaps the clearest definition of openness I can offer is this: If you are open, you don't need to know the ending of something at the beginning. When you allow yourself to be open to different outcomes and different steps along the way, expansiveness happens. You see things you wouldn't have seen otherwise, and you incorporate the things that fit into your pursuit. You also tend to enjoy things more, because the possibility of being surprised and delighted increases considerably.

I have a songwriter friend who is a pianist by training. One day, he picked up a guitar and started noodling on it, even though he knew very little about playing guitar. Soon, he started writing a song on the guitar and found that it sounded very different from his other songs. The simple fact that he was playing a different instrument, even though he didn't play it well, gave him a new musical language to work with. Since then, he's written some of his best songs on the guitar as well as the autoharp, the synthesizer, and even the harmonica. His work is better and has much more range because he was open to the new perspectives that came from playing different instruments. If he'd only stuck to the piano, he might never have written some of his most significant and affecting work.

Paul Simon speaks similarly to the value of openness in an interview he gave for the twenty-fifth anniversary release of his landmark album, *Graceland*, which he recorded with musicians in South Africa, along with musicians in several cities in America. Speaking of the title track, Simon noted that the song started with the drumbeat, which is reminiscent of a number of "traveling songs" from Sun Records recordings in the fifties. The track built through contributions from both African and American musicians, each of whom were interpreting the sounds they heard through their own cultural touch points. While the blend was unlike anything he was accustomed to hearing, Simon stayed open to it and this resulted in one of the signature moments on the album.

"The whole song really is just one sound evoking a response,"

Simon said during the interview, "and that eventually became a lyric that evoked—instead of being a South African subject or a political subject—it became a traveling song that had to do with the original sound which was the drums and Sun Records and Graceland. That's really the secret of world music is people are able to listen to each other and make associations and play their own music that sounds like it fits into another culture."

> People want more space to develop their own individual talents. They want more flexibility to explore their own interests and develop their own identities, lifestyles and capacities. They are more impatient with situations that they find stifling.
>
> —David Brooks, the *New York Times*

Life in permanent beta

Openness also leads to something that is increasingly essential in a world where change is defined in hours rather than eras: agility. If you're a member of the workforce, if you're a student contemplating the beginning of a career, or even if you're just trying to make the most of a hobby or an avocation, you're likely aware of how quickly life is swirling around you. The old cliché "The only constant is change" should be amended to "The only constant is *ever-increasing* change." In a world where this morning's accepted principles are this afternoon's hoary conventions, being closed simply isn't a workable option.

Reid Garrett Hoffman, the founder of the enormous networking site LinkedIn, has a very clear perspective on this gleaned from his entrepreneurial experience. He sees the work-force as a place where the contract between employer and em-ployee has changed profoundly. Where there was an unspoken agreement in previous generations that a hardworking, loyal, and trustworthy employee could expect career-long employment and regular promotions—and that in turn the employer could expect the employee to remain with the company indefinitely—employers now review their staffs much more critically, trim "fat" wherever possible, and seek every opportunity to outsource and automate, while employees switch jobs and even professions regularly.

Hoffman, who knows quite a bit about start-ups (in addition to LinkedIn, he was an early investor in Facebook and is on the boards of Zynga and Mozilla), believes the only healthy attitude for any person in the workforce to take today is that of a start-up. He calls this "the start-up of you," which, incidentally, is the title of his recent book, which he coauthored with entrepreneur Ben Casnocha. In an interview with Thomas Friedman, Hoffman and Casnocha said:

> Technology companies sometimes keep the "beta" label on software for a time after the official launch to stress that the product is not finished, so much as ready for the next batch of improvements. For entrepreneurs, finished is an F-word. Great companies are always evolving. Fin-ished ought to be an F-word for all of us. We are all works in progress. Each day presents an opportunity to learn more, do more, be more, grow more in our lives and ca-reers. You will need to adapt and evolve forever—that's per-manent beta.

In a piece he wrote about the book in the *New York Times*, Friedman added:

> Whatever you may be thinking when you apply for a job today, you can be sure the employer is asking this: Can this person add value every hour, every day—more than a worker in India, a robot or a computer? Can he or she help my company adapt by not only doing the job today but also reinventing the job for tomorrow? And can he or she adapt with all the change, so my company can adapt and export more into the fastest-growing global markets? In today's hyperconnected world, more and more companies cannot and will not hire people who don't fulfill those criteria.

What Hoffman, Casnocha, and Friedman are all advocating for is an increased use of the Essential of openness. When you are open, you are exponentially more adaptable, because you're paying attention to the signs that change is imminent or advisable. When you are open, you never consider yourself or your work to be a finished product, because you're always aware of how the world is shifting around you and how you need to shift with it. As the authors put it, you're in "permanent beta." And when you are open, you are significantly more likely to add value to any enterprise you are involved with, because you're specifically looking at the conditions that surround you and thinking about how you can create positive change in those conditions.

It's difficult to argue against Hoffman and Casnocha's thesis here. Given the velocity of change, not thinking like a start-up virtually guarantees that you'll be left on the sidelines, regardless

of your pursuit. It is also difficult to argue that these conditions
are temporary. The explosion of available information and the
metrics generated by this information are the tools fueling the
rapidity of change, and it is inconceivable that anything other
than a global cataclysm will cause employers and others to stop
using this information. Therefore, openness becomes not just an
advisable trait, but an indispensable one.

> I came in with a dream. But dreams are nebulous.
> They lack definition. That definition comes from
> the day-to-day, and the day-to-day is full of mis-
> takes and chance.
>
> —David Embree, CEO, Athletepath

Directed serendipity

In October 2011, Jim Collins, the best-selling author of *Good to
Great*, published an inspired essay in the *New York Times* about
the function of luck on hugely successful companies. In the piece,
Collins offers details from a nine-year study he performed on entrepreneurs who created companies that outperformed their industry by ten times (he calls them 10Xers). One of the people
studied was Bill Gates, who birthed Microsoft after the conflu-
ence of a series of "lucky" circumstances: He was born with a certain level of financial means, he went to a high school that had
access to a computer (unusual at the time), he came of age at the
precise moment when technology made the creation of a personal
computer possible, his friend Paul Allen introduced him to a

Popular Electronics article about microcomputers that led them to a discussion about converting the programming language BASIC into something that could be used on a personal computer, and he attended Harvard, which had the computer resources to allow him to develop his ideas.

One way of looking at what Bill Gates achieved is that he was incredibly fortunate. Everything fell into place to allow him to found Microsoft. However, as Collins points out, he was hardly the only person to whom these conditions applied. There were easily thousands of people with the same set of circumstances as Bill Gates. Why, then, is there only one Microsoft? Collins explains:

> The difference between Mr. Gates and similarly advantaged people is not luck. Mr. Gates went further, taking a confluence of lucky circumstances and creating a huge return on his luck. And this is the important difference.
>
> Luck, good and bad, happens to everyone, whether we like it or not. But when we look at the 10Xers, we see people like Mr. Gates who recognize luck and seize it, leaders who grab luck events and make much more of them.

What Collins is describing is openness taken to its most advantageous extreme. It's something I call "directed serendipity." The notion of directed serendipity is that you set out with some sort of plan, yet you have a complete willingness to allow outside input to take you someplace that aligns with your plan but that you could not have imagined ahead of time. I've never spoken with Bill Gates personally, but I'm relatively certain he wasn't imagining something on the scale of Microsoft when he first became interested in computers. However, he was open to the possibilities that might arise, and the serendipitous happened.

When you use the Essential of openness consistently, the serendipitous becomes not only possible, but even likely. Almost certainly it won't be on a Bill Gates level, but the chance of your getting more than you bargained for increases dramatically. I call this form of serendipity "directed" because you're taking an active role in it. You're moving yourself in a certain direction, but letting the spontaneous in.

I was recently speaking with someone who'd spent more than a decade in brand development for a large corporation. When she decided to go out on her own, she knew that she wanted to help small businesses with branding, and she built a basic list of services from the foundation of her corporate experience, expecting the bulk of her work to come from consulting. However, as she set out in this direction, she left herself open to evolving the business as it developed. Early on, a group of female small business owners asked her to speak at a function. This went so well that several additional speaking engagements followed by referral. As it turns out, she was quite good at this—something she was previously unaware of—and people happily paid to get her advice in this medium. Today, speaking represents more than half of her income, she's doing something she didn't even realize she loved, and her business has grown substantially because of it.

This is directed serendipity in a nutshell. Having a plan is a critical part of success, but being open to where you're truly meant to go with that plan is the key to a lasting endeavor.

Waiting to change the world

In the previous chapter, I talked about how there seem to be two forms of curiosity, an active one and a passive one. Openness also has active and passive forms. The active form is what we've been discussing throughout this chapter, adjusting your mindset and your reaction to input to welcome new possibilities. The passive form is captured succinctly by the word *patience*.

Patience in this context is a function of giving yourself the necessary time to discover things that might be extremely important to your situation. In some ways, this runs counter to Reid Hoffman's thesis that we all need to be able to operate with a start-up mentality, which often lacks sufficient information before demanding a reaction. However, patience as a long-form approach effectively complements active openness. In fact, using the kind of quick course correction that active openness supplies is best when also having the kind of patience that allows you to be open to major decisions when the time is right.

What's to be gained from employing patience? There might be no better example than the one provided by Jane Goodall in her decades-long study of chimpanzees. Goodall was a twenty-six-year-old fascinated with wild animals when Louis Leakey sent her to Gombe National Park, on the shore of Lake Tanganyika, in what we now know as Tanzania. She lacked a formal scientific education, but she had an intense passion for her subject and something that might have been exponentially more important: patience.

"I remember my first day," she told an interviewer, "looking up from the shore to the forest, hearing the apes and the birds, and smelling the plants, and thinking this is very, very unreal. Then I started walking through the forest and as soon as a chimp saw me, it would run away."

This would be the pattern for a long time. The chimps were aware that there was an "other" among them, and they had no interest in either interacting with that other or putting on a show for her. Goodall couldn't get any closer than five hundred yards before the chimps ran away. Her instincts told her that this would change if she waited them out, so she decided to establish a pattern of appearing in the same place—an elevation near a feeding area—every morning at the same time. Her belief was that if she became part of the chimps' environment, they'd ultimately adapt to her and begin behaving naturally in her presence.

This took profound patience on Goodall's part. The chimps continued to steer clear of her week after week, month after month. However, about a year after she first set up camp in Gombe, things began to change. The chimps started to allow her to come closer and began to act more naturally around her. It would be yet another year before they truly accepted her and started to interact with her, though most of this interaction at first involved lobbying for bananas.

Goodall's use of passive openness led to world-changing observations that a less patient participant might never have witnessed. It was she who first discovered that chimps use and even make tools. Until then, we believed that only humans were capable of such a thing. Louis Leakey summed up the implications of this when he responded to Goodall's discovery by writing, "Now we must redefine 'tool,' redefine 'man,' or accept chimpanzees as humans."

Goodall was also the first to find that chimps are omnivores rather than herbivores and that they even employ cunning hunting schemes, that they have distinct personalities and form close relationships, and that their social interaction and dysfunction in many ways mirror our own. Her work, which is one of the longest uninterrupted field studies in history, has had a dramatic effect not only on our understanding of the primate world but also on our understanding of ourselves. Yet it was only possible through the employment of passive openness. It is also an excellent example of something we discussed earlier: not knowing the ending at the beginning. Jane Goodall could not possibly have known how things would turn out or whether she would accomplish anything at all with this project. It is also clear that she didn't attempt to force an outcome. As a result, the "ending" was so much more than anyone could have imagined.

Jane Goodall is an outlier, even within her own community. For most of us, her exhibition of patience is supernatural. However, even as we acknowledge that most of us will never be anywhere near patient enough to observe something at a distance for more than a year before getting any tangible results or interacting with it in any meaningful way, we need to see the lesson in what Goodall's patience netted. Passive openness—the willingness to look for signs and changes that might not be immediately apparent—leads to some of the deepest discovery possible.

I have a friend who calls himself a "student" of his area of interest, which happens to be print media. What he means by this is that he's constantly observing the field and learning from the actions of others. Since he's actively involved in this field, he's always reacting to the changes in the business. However, he makes his big moves very deliberately and as a result of his pas-sively open observations. I don't think it is coincidental that he's one of the most creative people in his industry.

> Openness, patience, receptivity, solitude is
> everything.
>
> —Rainer Maria Rilke

Yes!

Maybe one of the best—and certainly one of the most entertaining—expressions of openness in action is improvisation. Improv troupes dazzle us with their ability to create stories on the spot while being spontaneously funny at the same time. It would be impossible to be this creative or this witty without be-ing very open.

Dave Morris is a storyteller, poet, teacher, and speaker who hails from Victoria, British Columbia. Mostly, though, he's an improviser, doing solo shows as well as performances with a sin-gle partner or an entire troupe. "Improvisation is about being an open person," he told me. "The first rule of improvisation is say-ing yes. When something comes to you, you say yes to it."

Morris illustrated the value of yes brilliantly during a pre-sentation he delivered at TEDxVictoria. He asked the audience to respond to each of his questions by saying yes.

"Do you want to tell a story with me?"

"Yes!"

"Is it a story about a knight?"

"Yes!"

"Is the knight wearing shining armor?"

"Yes!"

"Is he going to save a damsel?"

"Yes!"

"Is he being held by a dragon?"

"Yes!"

"Is the dragon breathing fire?"

"Yes!"

"Does he save her with courage and bravery?"

"Yes!"

"And do they live happily ever after?"

"Yes!"

Morris then applauded the crowd for their participation in an exciting story. After that, he told the audience that they were going to do the same sort of thing, but this time he wanted them to say no.

"Do you want to tell a story with me?"

"No!"

Morris put up his hands and said, "I'll just go; all right."

What Dave Morris did with this little exercise was identify the stark difference between being open and being closed. When you're open and saying yes, you can tell magical stories filled with adventure. When you're closed and saying no, you can't even get started.

"It's also about letting go of the things you had in your head," he said to me. "Being open to the things that are coming also involves a letting go. You can let go of these things you were thinking and say yes to the new thing. If you know the ending, that's where you're headed, and you're ignoring what's coming at you and just charging forward and knocking everything over. You need to be open to your partner and open to your audience. The more open you are to the audience and your partners, the more connected you are to your impulses, which is to say, yourself. You're more connected with who you are."

Morris teaches improvisation to both adults and schoolchildren. When he talks to them about openness, he explains that it's "a door, and you can come in or go out." Not only is it important to be open to allow input and ideas to get through to you, but you need to be open to sharing a part of yourself. "A big thing in improvisation is using your personal life and not being afraid to share—being open and letting things out as opposed to being open and letting things in. When you're doing a show by yourself, that's really all you have other than the audience.

"Improvising with a group is totally different. That's where the openness to let things happen comes in. Maybe you're playing out something from your real life, like your girlfriend just broke up with you, and you're playing it out exactly as it happened. Then another member of the group comes in with something that didn't happen and you have to let go of your version of events and move on with this fictitious story. I teach people that what happens on the stage is the only truth. What happens in your head is just a possibility. You need to let go of all the possibilities and focus on what's actually happening in the story."

This underscores a point I've made elsewhere in this chapter—that openness allows for the creation of things that you never could have created if you'd stayed closed. Our lives are so much like the stories being invented on improv stages all over the world. If we share ourselves and remain open to other ways that our stories might go, we are likely to create something exponentially richer and more rewarding than if we'd just stayed in our own heads. For Morris, if he'd simply spun out his breakup tale, he might have gotten a bit of audience sympathy. Letting the story go where others wanted to help him take it, though, allowed him the opportunity for a standing ovation. This is true for each of us, whether our "stage" is a conference room, a retail store, a school board meeting, or anyplace else we're doing something that matters to us.

When I mentioned to Morris that so much of what he teaches to his improvisation students applies to life in general, he responded, "Well, of course; life is improvised."

chapter three

The Essential of Sensuality

ONE WOULD LIKE to believe that anyone we entrust with cutting into our bodies would have all of their senses in optimal working order. Our bodies, after all, are rather precious to us. However, for some surgeons, this isn't the case at all. Instead, they achieve superior results by eschewing one of their senses for outsize benefits from another.

Adam Fechner is an infertility specialist with Hackensack-UMC Mountainside, in Montclair, New Jersey, and a robotic surgeon using the da Vinci Surgical System. When he was a resident, robotic surgical systems were still relatively new and, as he told me, "A lot of surgeons ran the other way" because they felt it was too foreign to their medical experience. However, Fechner realized that the system could be quite beneficial for certain procedures, and he sought the opportunity to refine this skill.

"Standard abdominal surgery is known as laparotomy," he explained. "You make a big abdominal incision, and once you do, you can feel everything with your hands. The view you have, unless you're using a microscope, is a couple of feet away looking into the incision with lights."

While laparotomy brought the surgeon in very close physical contact with the patient, the procedure led to long hospital stays, extremely long recuperation times, and considerable, noticeable scars.

"From that, it moved to laparoscopy, where you could put a couple of small holes in the patient, and put a camera in one of them and the instruments in the other. You're still standing next to the patient, and you're still holding the other ends of the instruments. You move the camera to what you want to see, and you use the instruments to cut. You still touch things and see how they feel because you're essentially holding a stick and you can poke at things. This allows you to tell how the tissue responds."

Laparoscopic procedures decreased hospital stays, with many patients going home the same day and getting back to their regular lives within a week. In addition, the scars were tiny and barely noticeable. Bikinis were still an option for those to whom bikinis were an option before the operation. Laparoscopy brought with it limitations, though. "Laparoscopic instruments can basically turn or open and close, but there are no wrist motions," Fechner said. "If you have a more intricate surgery or something where you're going to be doing a lot of sewing, it becomes more difficult."

Robotic surgery combines key advantages of laparotomy and laparoscopy. The surgeon's range of motion is as great as it is in open surgery, but the recovery times and scarring are similar to that in laparoscopy.

"What happens with a robot is that you still have just a few holes—usually five—you put the camera through one of them and it is three-dimensional and high-definition, and it is more magnified. The benefit is that rather than standing at the end of the instrument, you bring in the robot and control it from a console. You can make finer movements with it and the robot corrects for tremors."

Robotic surgery also gives the surgeon access to another set of arms, and with it an entirely new level of sensory input. "With laparoscopy, you have two hands, so you need to hold the camera with one hand and the instruments in the other. With the robot, you have control over four arms. You have control of the camera with one of these and three others that can have three instruments in them. I'll have a left hand that always has a grasper, and in my right hand I can toggle between retracting and a scissor. So if there's a piece of bowel in the way, I can grab it with one of my right arms, pull it out of the way, lock it in place, and then go in with my other right arm and still have two hands to operate—and still control the camera."

Fechner acknowledges that there was a fairly sizable learning curve associated with such a change. While there are distinct advantages to having an extra set of arms, navigating through a surgeon's environment with these required some adjustment, as I suppose would be true for any of us who suddenly had the use of two more limbs. It was all too easy to find instruments banging against each other or acting as a disruptive presence in the patient's system.

Perhaps the biggest sensory challenge, though, came from the lack of tactile feedback. Robotic surgery *feels* dramatically

different to surgeons, because their hands are no longer at the
ends of the instruments. "When I'm removing fibroids from a
uterus, the uterus is like muscle, so it feels like any muscle, and
the fibroids are dense and firm. If we did the surgery open, I
could feel the uterus to find out if there are any other fibroids in
there. With laparoscopy, if we felt a bulge we could poke it with
the instrument. With the robot, we don't have that."

The sense of touch is diminished considerably in robotic surgery. What compensates for this, seeming to take this sort of
surgery up to another level, are the extraordinary visuals available through the 3-D high-def camera.

"Your sense of sight takes over for your sense of touch. You
see how the tissue responds to the touch of the robotic instrument, and you figure out what's there. Your sense of touch is essentially gone, but because of the images, it's almost like you can
feel it even though you can't. You may see a bulge in the uterus
and you don't know if it's a fibroid or a normal bulge, but by
touching it with the instrument you can see how much give it
has. It's like if you have a balloon filled with water and a balloon
filled with sand. If someone else is poking it and you're just
watching, you can tell by how much it gives which balloon has
which. The visualization gives you a connection you wouldn't
otherwise have. You're seeing anatomy like no one has ever seen
before. It would be like putting binoculars on your eyes during
an open procedure."

For a surgeon, the senses of sight and touch are inarguably
the most important. With robotic systems like da Vinci, one of
those critical senses is all but eliminated; however, the other is
heightened to such a degree that the entire process can be better.

It is a fascinating testament to what is possible when we are conscious of the way we employ our Essential of sensuality and strive to make the best possible use of our senses.

> The words or the language, as they are written or spoken, do not seem to play any role in my mechanism of thought. The psychical entities which seem to serve as elements in thought are certain signs and more or less clear images which can be "voluntarily" reproduced and combined. . . . This combinatory play seems to be the essential feature in productive thought before there is any connection with logical construction in words or other kinds of signs which can be communicated to others.
>
> —Albert Einstein

Envisioning Yeltsin

Simply put, sensuality is feeling your own experience of your own experience. It's allowing yourself the highest level of awareness of what is going on inside and around you.

We all face a strong temptation to skim over the surface of our lives because that is the easier course. After all, you're much less likely to bog down in something unpleasant if you avoid all but a minimum of stimuli. However, when you allow your senses to partake of the world in full, you are undeniably alive and living in an authentic way. Truly sensual people live an emotional and sensory roller coaster—and they wouldn't want anything other than that.

They understand that their senses are invaluable assets that allow them to interact with the world at the richest possible level and identify the experiences that feel absolutely right to them. They have a better sense of their circumstances and how to heighten those circumstances, because they are truly paying attention.

When we turn the dial up on our senses, we experience things internally and externally that we would not be privy to otherwise. Turning our senses outward, we encounter a perspective on the world that isn't visible at the surface level. When we listen to what people are saying, watch for patterns and inconsistencies, and truly feel the world around us, it is as though our environment is suddenly snapping into focus. It reminds me of the Magic Eye images that were so popular in the nineties. These autostereograms appear to be one thing or a mélange of several things, but when you teach yourself to take a certain approach to looking at them, entirely new three-dimensional images emerge from a flat page. The Magic Eye books are so popular because they offer a unique experience—the ability to see things in a richer way. This is what sensuality offers us. What appears to be one thing on the surface—something unknowable or uninteresting—takes on new levels of texture and fascination when you look deeper.

I had a breakthrough experience with this many years ago when I was doing a project for the U.S. Department of Defense. Boris Yeltsin was rising to prominence in the Russian government, and American officials asked me to write an assessment of him so they could try to understand whom they were dealing with. I spent months on the assignment, collecting every piece of data I could find about him—his history, his biography, the details of his political life. However, in spite of all of this work, I couldn't get a handle on him. I'd never met the man, and all I had was a series of data points to work with. I couldn't engage my senses, because I didn't have enough to engage them and no real method with which to start.

I was finally able to track down one of Yeltsin's biographers, someone who knew him very, very well. I asked this man to tell me a couple of things that distinctly defined Yeltsin for him. He had observed Yeltsin keenly, and he answered me with two things I had uncovered nowhere else. The first was that Yeltsin loved playing volleyball and that he took uncommon pleasure in spiking a ball on an opponent. The other was that whenever Yeltsin got out of a car, he bolted out of it rather than waiting for his driver to open the door for him.

With this information in hand, along with the data points I already had, the three-dimensional image emerged. What became clear to me was that Yeltsin sought to destabilize his immediate environment—rising up and dropping a blow on an opponent; emerging at his destination with unexpected suddenness. Once I had this observation, I saw it everywhere in his actions. In this case, I relied on the biographer's Essential of sensuality to help the picture emerge. I have little doubt, though, that if I'd had direct access to Yeltsin for any period, I would have come away with the same thing.

Making full use of your senses promises this level of insight, whether you're characterizing heads of state, getting a better grip on your work environment, trying to identify where a relationship is going, or even just attempting to decide the best use of a few hours of leisure time. It allows you to go beyond the data points available at the surface level, and when you dig deeper to understand something, your perceptions of that something accrue to your benefit.

Feeling his way to a flop

Dick Fosbury was a flop.

For most of his Oregon high school athletic career, the only heights Fosbury reached were those of mediocrity. Back in the early sixties, high jumpers used either a scissors kick—a set of movements that involves jumping over the bar one leg at a time— or a straddle, which requires jumping and rolling (in midair) in such a way that your body clears the bar. Neither of these techniques worked effectively for Fosbury, who has admitted that he wasn't a naturally gifted athlete. Incapable of clearing five feet four inches, he had little hope of competing with the stronger high jumpers in his state.

Instead of Fosbury turning out to be a flop in the world of track, though, his name became synonymous with the word *flop*—for all the right reasons. Realizing he had a surprising ability to switch from running to leaping, the sixteen-year-old Fosbury decided to try going over the bar headfirst, faceup, and backward. No one around him had ever seen anyone do this before, and a local newspaper wrote that he looked like "a fish flopping in a boat." It might all have been comical except for one thing: It worked brilliantly. By the time he graduated, Fosbury was the second-best high school high jumper in Oregon.

That was only the beginning, though. He soon won the National Junior Championships, which led to a scholarship to

Oregon State. However, he saved his best flop for the biggest stage, winning the 1968 Olympic gold medal in the high jump and setting a world record in the process. In so doing, he reinvented the sport. U.S. coach Payton Jordan was quoted as saying, "Kids imitate champions. If they try to imitate Fosbury, he'll wipe out an entire generation of high jumpers because they all will have broken necks." But before long, the vast majority of high jumpers were flopping to success, and they continue to do so today. In the 2012 Olympics, Ivan Ukhov took the gold medal in the high jump by leaping over a bar set nearly seven feet ten inches off the ground. He of course used the flop.

As I was putting my thoughts together for this book, my mind went to Dick Fosbury quite often. His story is instructive for many reasons, but perhaps none more so than showing how much we can achieve—and how fulfilled we can feel—when we pay careful attention to our senses. While I'm sure Fosbury worked hard and took to being coached, his story is not that time-honored classic about someone who refused to give up and who finally found a mentor to help him get to the next level. Instead, it's about someone who realized—quite surprisingly—that his body had a resource he hadn't previously recognized, and that by using this resource, he could excel at something that mattered to him. Fosbury understood the fundamentals of high jumping, but he also understood that he couldn't be a very good high jumper unless he went completely against convention and made the most of his ability to switch quickly from running to leaping. Instead of beating himself up over his inability to get over the bar the old-fashioned way or trying in vain to succeed until he collapsed in a heap, he listened to what his senses were telling him: Try doing this a different way.

Several generations of high jumpers are glad he was paying attention.

Just one more thing

Whenever I think of sensuality, I inevitably come around to thinking about Lt. Columbo, the fictional television police detective played by Peter Falk for more than three decades. Columbo looked like anything other than an ace investigator. He wore rumpled clothing, he seemed easily distracted, and he tended to pursue his cases in the most circuitous manner imaginable. However, he was uncannily effective—because he was making full use of his senses.

"The attitude and behavior . . . are all an act," journalist Dennis Bounds says on the Museum of Broadcast Communications website. "Columbo is not confused but acutely aware, like a falcon circling its prey, waiting for a moment of weakness. Columbo bumbles about, often interfering with the activities of the uniformed police and gathering what seem to be the most unimportant clues. All the while he constantly pesters the person he has pegged as his central suspect.

"At first even the murderer is amused at the lieutenant's style and usually seems inclined to assume that if this is the best the Los Angeles police can offer, the murder will never be found out. But whenever the suspect seems to be rid of the lieutenant, Columbo turns with a bemused remark, something like, 'Oh, there's just one more thing. . . .' By the end of the episode, Columbo has taken an apparently minor discrepancy in the murderer's story and wound it into the noose with which to hang the suspect."

Columbo is a paragon of sensuality. Knowing that the best information often lies well beneath the surface, he doesn't attack a case by going straight at the facts. Instead, he settles into it, opening his senses to what he might pick up: an observation here, an intonation there, an inconsistency somewhere else. "How do I solve a case?" Columbo says in one episode. "I follow my nose. I want to get the scent, the smell of a case. How else would you solve a case? You go to the oldest and fastest part of the brain."

This notion of the "oldest and fastest part of the brain" (Paul MacLean calls it the "reptilian brain" in his triune brain theory) gets to something very closely associated with sensuality: instinct. Your senses often alert you to things long before you can consciously think of them. In Columbo's case, instinct is the sense that a sign might lead to a killer or that a suspect's story doesn't add up. As a character says in one of the *Columbo* episodes, "You pass yourself off as a puppy in a raincoat happily running around the yard digging holes all up in the garden, only you're laying a minefield and wagging your tail."

One of the ways in which Columbo disarms suspects (and often infuriates those working a case with him) is by appearing to be bumbling around. He appears to be focusing on small and seemingly tangential things while others do the heavy lifting, yet this aimlessness—which is actually his turning himself over to his senses—always leads him to the solution. The message here is that we might all benefit from doing a bit more bumbling—at least of the Columbo variety. There's much to be gained from letting the situation and the environment direct you. Answers—which for most of us have nothing to do with solving crimes and much to do with finding the next meaningful thing to do—often come when you allow yourself to get a sense of the landscape and then think, "Oh, there's just one more thing."

> You don't have relationships and you don't listen and your senses go dull. You don't really know what you think about something. What do I think about that? Do I really like that person? Do I really wanna continue putting time into that relationship? Or is it just what I think I should do? And you're not living your life in the moment, you know? Cathy's done everything well because she's kept it very safe. But she hasn't really done anything very deeply.
>
> —Laura Linney on her character Cathy from *The Big C*

Running a regular "systems check"

Sensuality means feeling, listening to, and observing the world and others. It also means doing the same with yourself. Paying attention to what your senses are telling you about your own condition allows a level of self-awareness that is invaluable. As you know, each of the other four Essentials works in the service of having a fully developed self-story, but self-story is on a much grander scale than what I'm addressing here. Inner sensuality allows you to run an ongoing "systems check" that lets you know when you're in need of an emotional or even physical course correction.

Anna Quindlen, a Pulitzer Prize–winning journalist and *New York Times* best-selling author, underscored the life-changing value of inner sensuality during an interview with National

Public Radio for her 2012 book, *Lots of Candles, Plenty of Cake*. Asked by *Fresh Air*'s Terry Gross about troubles she had with alcohol in the past, Quindlen responded, "In any battle between me and alcohol, alcohol always won. At a certain point, I just realized, 'This isn't going to work for you in the long run.' I looked at my kids and I thought, 'When you drink, your personality tends to change over the course of it. So you have one glass of wine and you're kind of jolly, and you have two and you get quieter, and you have three and maybe you get a little spiky.' I think kids need as much consistency as possible and I don't think a kid should have three or four different iterations of Mom during the course of a given evening, and that's why I stopped."

Quindlen's perceptiveness about herself is both laudable and instructive, because it shows us how much of an effect inner sensuality can have on one's life. Had Quindlen been paying less attention to the ways in which her state of mind morphed when she drank, she might never have stopped doing so and she might have done her children the disservice she managed to avoid.

Self-awareness can be used for relatively more mundane purposes as well. Do you speak too quickly when you're nervous? Do you tend to overeat when you're stressed? Do certain environmental conditions make you edgy, defensive, inhibited, or voluble? Do you "change" around a particular type of person or when you're in different situations? If you're regularly listening to yourself, feeling your internal rhythms, and watching your behavior, there's a far better chance that you'll feel more comfortable in your own skin. In this way, sensuality—and specifically inner sensuality—has tremendous practical value.

> I've always sensed as I entered a book that things
> began to happen just outside the range of the
> immediate action. It's simply the way my mind
> works. There's very little sense of a logic behind it.
>
> —Don DeLillo

Coming off the page

As you've probably picked up on by now, I have particular affection for novelists, because I think the best of them teach us so much and offer us illuminated paths to follow. They also help to illustrate sensuality well, because they employ it in a distinctive and instructive way. While readers might find a novelist's plotting skills or prose style captivating, most emotionally connect with a work of fiction only if the novelist can create realistic and relatable characters. Doing so is a refined talent and requires observing the world at an intense level.

Caroline Leavitt is the *New York Times* best-selling author of *Pictures of You* and the recent *Is This Tomorrow,* and she is a senior instructor at the UCLA Extension Writers' Program. Known for the rich way in which she evokes her characters, she has studied this part of her craft carefully and has a unique perspective on it.

"The first thing I do is go through Google Images," she told me when I asked how she began the process of creating a character. "I have to find a picture of what I think the character looks like. It's not so much what they physically look like as it is the expression on the faces of the people in the photographs. On my wall right now, I have a picture of a man who looks like a teacher, but he's frowning, and that frown to me is interesting because I feel that it leads to story. I have another picture of a young girl who is just staring into the camera, and I like that because I feel that the stare leads to story as well. I don't necessarily know what these characters are doing at this point or what they're going to do, but it's important to me to have their pictures hanging up by my computer so I feel that I'm living with them and they're becoming more visible to me.

"There's a Facebook page, Humans of New York, put up by a photographer. They're the best photographs because they're real people and they don't look airbrushed and they're all interesting. It's just what a novelist needs."

What Leavitt is looking for in these pictures has little to do with the physical attributes of the faces and a great deal to do with the emotion the photographs convey. Her search for a picture to represent an elderly woman she wanted to include in one of her novels led her to an image of someone with her hands on her face. By studying the image and bringing her observations about life to bear on it, Leavitt saw something about how the woman carried herself that suggested that she was very stylish and that she'd gone through a great deal of trouble to look interesting. This took the character Leavitt was writing about in new directions.

The observations that novelists make to bring a character to life require a level of understanding about those characters that never appears on the page. "A lot of the work I do on the characters doesn't see the light of day. I'll write lists of what her favorite food is, what music she likes, what she was like as a kid, whether she believed in Santa Claus or believes in God. It's a really long, involved process. It usually takes me four to six months to figure it all out. I write twenty-page outlines of what I think these characters want, what they know coming into the story, what they don't know that's really hurting them and hurting other people, and what they will know in the end. It's important for me to write these whole-life biographies even if I'll never use most of it.

"I tell my writing students at UCLA to go on the dating site eHarmony. They have a questionnaire that you have to fill out to see who you would be good for, and it's really inclusive. They ask you all kinds of questions like, 'Do you like to be alone?' or 'What happens when you're at a party?' As you fill it out, you're starting to create a character."

Another component of character creation is understanding the deeper levels of the character's motivations. "I took a screenwriting course with John Truby. He talks about the moral component of the characters. He says that it's not enough that every character just wants something for himself or herself. They also have to have what he calls a 'moral need.' I might have a character who wants to stop drinking. That's his psychological need. Then I have to go deeper and think, 'What's the thing that he's lacking that he needs in order to have a fuller life?' So maybe he needs to stop drinking so he can be a better husband. I do that and then I go right to the Rolling Stones' 'You Can't Always Get What You Want.' I figure out that the character loves something, and I'm not going to give it to him, but I'm going to give him something he needs.

"I tell my students that every character has to have a ghost. The ghost is the backstory, the thing that happened in the past that made them who they are. It really haunts them and they're going to have to deal with that ghost in some way or another. To me, that's what makes an interesting story. If you start out haunted to begin with, then whatever you do after that is more interesting because you're more likely to screw yourself up to get wherever you want to get."

As careful and comprehensive as Leavitt is with this process, she, like most serious novelists I've spoken with over the years, can't define exactly how she knows that the character has become three-dimensional. "I know in the moment when I've created a character that feels real. I'll be writing and suddenly it feels like the character is taking over and making his or her own decisions. It always takes months and months to get to that, but when it happens, it's amazing because then the character is alive. If the character is not alive, I can write a scene where he is thinking about jumping off a building and I'm very conscious of being the writer and not being moved by it or nervous about it. But if the character is alive and I'm writing that scene, I get nervous and I have an emotional response. The best times are when I'm writing something and it moves me so much that I cry."

The kind of careful work that novelists do to create characters has considerable implications for all of us. In order for a character to feel real to readers, the novelist needs to employ the Essential of sensuality in an acute way. Skimming the surface is strictly prohibited during this exercise. A novelist must dig far below the surface to get at the core components of humanity. And just as doing so allows a novel's characters to take a meaningful place in our imaginations, when we make the most of our sensuality, we "come off the page" in the stories of our lives in a more real way.

The process Caroline Leavitt describes is one of endless

observation—from identifying the emotion behind a face in a photograph to perceiving what a love of vindaloo might say about an individual to searching for one's personal ghost—and it is a process that delivers substantial rewards. When people spend the time to carefully examine themselves and the world around them, they intersect and interact with their environment in ways that are otherwise impossible, and they lend something approaching that much-desired literary majesty to their existence.

chapter four

The Essential of Paradox

THE JAZZ AGE was a heady time in American popular culture. This dramatically new form of music, which coincided with the mass marketing of radio, expanded minds and imaginations with its near-total reinvention of song structure, and excited libidos with its simmering sexuality. Artists like Louis Armstrong, Duke Ellington, Count Basie, and Bessie Smith gained levels of popularity previously unknown to black artists in the United States, as audiences both black and white found themselves captivated by sounds they'd never heard before.

While jazz was exciting enough when played through a small speaker in one's living room, live jazz truly electrified. There were jazz clubs in many cities, but the place with the hottest nightspots during this era was New York, specifically Harlem. At venues like the Cotton Club and the Savoy Ballroom, jazz fans could catch the biggest stars in an elegant setting, flirting with a dangerous lifestyle in relative safety deep into the night.

One place where the party ran into the early hours of the

morning was Wells Supper Club. Realizing that the demand was there, Wells started to leave the kitchen open until closing. However, as the evening wore on, diners seemed increasingly confused about what to order. It was way past suppertime, but it was far too early for breakfast. Joseph Wells appreciated the dilemma and saw that it fit neatly with one of his own: what to do with the fried chicken that was inevitably left over at the end of supper service. He began to offer late-night diners a new menu item that combined dinner and breakfast: chicken and waffles. This became the signature dish at Wells, and soon this combination evolved into an international sensation.

The provenance of chicken and waffles is subject to some disagreement, maybe going as far back as the eighteenth century, but the widespread popularity of the dish traces directly back to Wells, who seemed to understand that blending breakfast and dinner could create something unique and unforgettable. Wells didn't allow himself to be constrained by the conventions of either mealtime. Instead, he embraced the power of "and." He made memorable and appetite-changing use of his Essential of paradox.

> Things are always advancing now, getting better.
> Sometimes for the worse.
>
> —A focus group respondent

The Snodgrass Prize for American Humor?

As a writer just beginning to establish his literary career, Samuel Clemens played with the idea of several pseudonyms, including

W. Epaminondas Adrastus Perkins and Thomas Jefferson Snod-grass. Eventually, he reached back to his years as an apprentice river pilot—and to paradox—for his inspiration.

In the days of steamboats, it was common for the crew to use a long measuring stick to determine the depth of the water in fathoms (a fathom is approximately six feet). For a steamboat, a depth of twelve feet was necessary for safe passage. Therefore, there would always be someone in the crew responsible for mak-ing sure that the fathom indicator never dropped below the sec-ond mark, or "mark twain." In this context, mark twain stood as the dividing line between safety and danger.

Given Clemens's penchant for contradiction in his writing—he regularly threw cultures, mores, and ethics into relief, and his work often shifted from the broadly comic to the poignantly thoughtful—it's likely that he chose his nom de plume to under-score his fascination with paradox. One might imagine him saying that with this name he saw himself as someone who would walk the line between what was accepted in polite com-pany and what was only discussed in whispers. By adopting the persona of Mark Twain, Samuel Clemens seemed to be announc-ing to the world that his writing was going to be living on the edge and that he was both cognizant and appreciative of life's paradoxes.

He also created for us a context in which to understand paradox—two seemingly opposed things, for instance safety and danger, that when combined create something genuine and dis-tinctive.

The purity of contradiction

Many people think of paradoxes as problems that need to be solved or resolved. Do we embrace the speed with which the world is changing or drop off the grid? Do we break the rules or stick with the status quo? Do we have breakfast or dinner?

In reality, though, paradox is a gift, an invaluable asset for dealing with life, an Essential. It's unlikely that there was ever a time when our existence fit neatly into categories, but it certainly doesn't work that way now. Nothing is all one piece; everything is a mash-up of this and that. Complexity is a given in everything, from the work we do to the leaders we follow, from the hobbies we enjoy to the entertainment we experience. Considering the ubiquity of information, there is always a flood of data available to us, much of it contradictory.

Frankly, resolving this situation doesn't seem like a realistic option. Fortunately, it isn't remotely necessary or for that matter even remotely advisable, because embracing paradox offers us the opportunity to truly be ourselves. In paradox lies the chance to go past the restraints of the here and near to the exploratory freedom of not exactly knowing but searching. It's a way past the obvious given. It's a way toward the next. Paradox recognizes complexity— the absence of the simple and the linear—not as a threat, but as a challenge to help you find your way to something new. To imitate Dr. Seuss for a moment, it might be the *you-est* of the Essentials.

During the 2012 South by Southwest music, film, and interactive festival, Bruce Springsteen delivered a keynote address. During that speech, he offered the following advice to the musicians in the audience:

Don't take yourself too seriously, and take yourself as seriously as death itself.

Don't worry. Worry your ass off.

Have unclad confidence, but doubt. It keeps you awake and alert.

Believe you are the baddest ass in town—and you suck! It keeps you honest.

Be able to keep two completely contradictory ideas alive and well inside your heart and head at all times. If it doesn't drive you crazy, it will make you strong.

In this address, Springsteen relates several paradoxes that any ambitious person faces. Yes, it is important that you not get caught up in your own importance, *and* at the same time, it's critical that you honor the importance of what you are doing. If not, you'll be either insufferable or irrelevant. You can't allow concerns about what might go wrong to consume you, *and* you need to be diligent always. If not, you won't be able to get out of bed in the morning, or you'll leave yourself open to horrible mistakes. It's essential that you believe in yourself, *and* you need to question everything you do. If not, you won't have the strength to persevere, or you won't continually strive for improvement. You need to feel as though you're the master of all you survey *and* that you're barely worthy of attention. If not, you won't inspire others or you'll be too full of yourself to matter.

The last message that Springsteen passes along here is the essence of paradox. Embracing paradox is about acknowledging that your best path through life might be to manifest one ideal *and* its seeming opposite. It's also about not letting it drive you crazy. Many people live comfortably and even triumphantly in the land of paradox. Here are three:

Ben Folds

"When we started in Chapel Hill, NC in 1994," reads the copy in a promotional video for the 2012 Ben Folds Five album *The Sound of the Life of the Mind*, "it was the heyday of grunge music. It was all guitars and no harmonies. Many said we didn't know what we were doing. They were right. And in 2012, we still don't. But we're not alone now, because in 2012, NOBODY knows what they're doing."

Ben Folds is a musical artist who seems in full control of his Essential of paradox. Consider the fact that the band that first brought him to prominence, Ben Folds Five, has *three* members. Or that this favorite of alternative music fans recently served as a judge on a distinctly mainstream network television vocal competition, *The Sing-Off*. Or that one of his most popular compositions, "Rockin' the Suburbs," is written from the perspective of a middle-class white guy complaining about how tough it is to be so ordinary.

Unlike artists of earlier generations, Folds doesn't seem constrained by pop music conventions. He's a piano rocker who brings to mind singer-songwriters like Elton John and Billy Joel, but he doesn't allow himself to be pigeonholed. "He has written many silly-sounding songs about serious topics," says *Imprint Magazine* in a piece about Folds, "such as the song 'Effington,' which is about the conformity and confinement of small towns, and 'Bitch Went Nuts,' which is about the trials of breaking up. Ben has also been known to sprinkle his repertoire with a paradoxically polar array of songs, mixing gravely serious songs like 'Brick' (which is about an abortion) with songs such as 'Hiroshima,' which is about falling off the stage and contains the lyric 'I waved hello to the crowd as I busted ass off the front of the stage.' "

Where Folds most notably embraces paradox is in his lyrics. In "The Luckiest," a tender love song shifts in the third verse to the story of a couple in their nineties who died within a couple of days of each other. Love songs don't usually address death in old age (it would be difficult to imagine Cole Porter or Paul McCartney going in that direction), but Folds not only made the paradox work; he made it come off as deeply romantic—so much so that "The Luckiest" has become a popular song for the first dance at weddings.

What Folds appears to have uncovered with this and many of his other songs is that there's an emotional connection to be made in the seeming paradox of sincerity and irony. His song "Gracie," written for his daughter, includes many of the sentiments of new fathers (her being an inseparable part of him, his unwillingness to move while she sleeps in his arms for fear of waking her), but it also includes the line "You'll be a lady soon, but until then you gotta do what I say." A verse from "There's Always Someone Cooler Than You" begins, "Life is wonderful. Life is beautiful. We're all children of one big universe," and then ends, "So you don't have to be a chump." Even one of his most emotionally wrenching songs, "Evaporated," includes the torch song standby "I poured my heart out," but resolves it with "It evaporated." In every case, the irony heightens the sincerity rather than diminishing it. What Folds seems to understand so well is that pulling back on the sentiment rather than rushing headlong into it has the effect of deepening the emotional response from listeners.

Louis C.K.

Thinking about paradox makes me think of comedy. Comedy is in so many ways about paradox. We laugh because something surprises us, and the reason it surprises us is often that the comic has presented us with an ironic perspective we haven't considered before.

Paradox is a foundation of the comedy of Louis C.K. A stand-up comic, actor, and writer who made the 2012 Time 100, *Time* magazine's list of the one hundred most influential people in the world, he's best known for his HBO specials and his FX television series, *Louie*. *Rolling Stone* called the latter "a critically adored hit that blurs together cringe comedy, poignant drama, bathroom humor, slapstick gore and surrealist flights of fancy: It's impossible to say exactly what you're watching, and impossible to pull your eyes away." They said of C.K. (which is a variation on his family name, Szekely), "He's perfected a unique mixture of abject self-loathing, crushing pessimism, wide-eyed curiosity and, here and there, glimmers of hard-won sweetness."

Louie employs paradox in ways that both make us laugh and touch us deeply. In one episode, he takes his daughters to meet his ninety-nine-year-old great-aunt so they can learn about the past and have an innocent, old-fashioned time in a rural house with a sweet old woman. (One of the foundational paradoxes of the show is that Louis is a borderline misanthrope who adores his children.) It turns out that the aunt is a bigot whose racist comments upset the kids and leave Louis with a series of moral dilemmas over how to deal with this with his children.

Another episode opens with Louis and several of his comedian friends playing poker and talking trash to one another. The humor gets coarser and coarser, ultimately touching down on gay sex. In the midst of the one-upmanship that ensues, the one gay member of the group explains the etymology of a particularly offensive gay epithet. Though he has been as ribald as the others during this exchange, C.K. reacts with sincere curiosity and genuine concern over the casualness with which they have been throwing the term around, even implying that he might stop using it in his politically incorrect act. True to the show's ironic nature, though, another character then directs the term in jest at the gay character, and the gay character kisses him on the forehead, defusing the moment.

C.K. turns to paradox consistently in his stand-up routines. "Everything that makes you happy is going to end at some point, and nothing good ends well," he said in one stand-up routine on *Louie*. "It's like, if you buy a puppy, you're bringing it home to your family saying, 'Hey, look, everyone, we're all gonna cry soon. Look at what I brought home. I brought home us crying in a few years. Here we go. Countdown to sorrow with a puppy.'"

"Divorce is always good news," he says in his concert film *Hilarious*. "I know that sounds weird, but it's true because no good marriage has ever ended in divorce."

For C.K., employing his Essential of paradox is an effective way to get laughs. Like all influential artists, though, he has greater ambitions. Paradox allows him to turn the world on its ear and force us to look at it in new ways.

"I think it's really interesting to test what people think is right or wrong," he said in a 2011 interview, "and I can do that in both directions, so sometimes it's in defense of the common person against the rich that think they're entitled to this shit, but also the idea that everybody has to get handouts and do whatever they want so that there's not supposed to be any struggle in life is also a lot of horseshit. Everything that people say is testable."

Ferran Adrià

One of Ferran Adrià's stated goals is to bewilder. For twenty-five years, he operated El Bulli, the three-Michelin-star restaurant in Spain that was widely considered the world's greatest. It was also one of the most inaccessible. In its final year, more than two million people tried to be among the eight thousand diners who would be allowed to sit there for a meal. They sought reservations so they could experience food that was available nowhere else. They wanted to get into El Bulli so they could taste paradox.

Adrià opened the doors to El Bulli only six months out of every year. The other six were devoted to working with his team to develop new dishes, since he threw out his menu every time the restaurant went on hiatus. The break was necessary because at the core of El Bulli's gastronomy were two paradoxes, both of which required extensive invention to create. One was visual—a glowing "lollipop" made of fish; caviar created from olive oil; a liquid ravioli. The other was gustatory—the mind expected something in the mound of "air" on the plate other than pure lemon juice; the "spaghetti" was actually parmesan cheese.

While Adrià seeks to bewilder with his culinary creations, those creations are never simply tricks. He and his chefs spend endless hours deconstructing food and seeking new ways to present an ingredient not because they want to turn it into something it is not, but because they want to turn it into the ultimate version of itself.

"Ferran is an emperor," reads a recent piece about him, "a quixotic emperor of illogical, counterintuitive cuisine. You can see that he is for real, he's seriously dedicated to taking these food transformations and reinventions as far as they will go. He's the Deconstructor of Food. He is a paradox, part genius, part crackpot, which is usually part of genius, of invention. Is it that lunacy that allows him to go as far out on a limb as he has and end with a gastronomy game changer, a new way for one of the world's oldest activities, feeding people?"

For Adrià himself, the purpose of his paradoxical creations is to make the ordinary and necessary experience of eating as transcendent as he can—to tease out the deepest experience from something so fundamental to our existence. Perhaps this is why one could regularly find diners crying tears of joy or taking long, rapturous moments for themselves while savoring their meals at El Bulli.

"Painting, music, movies, sculpture, theater, everything—we can survive without it," he has said. "You have to eat, or else you die. Food is the only obligatory emotion."

What we learn from Ben Folds, Louis C.K., and Ferran Adrià is that embracing paradox is a vital path toward refining a persona. Each of their stories includes the word *and* in a prominent place; their uniqueness is defined by the ways in which they've combined seemingly contradictory motifs. Paradox, when productively employed, makes you stand out from all around you.

> Part of me suspects that I'm a loser, and the other part of me thinks I'm God Almighty.
>
> —John Lennon

Downshifting and upshifting at the same time

Even our nervous system pays homage to paradox. Within the involuntary, or autonomic, side of our nervous system, we have a sympathetic and parasympathetic component. The sympathetic nervous system essentially helps us to get through crises. When we're in high-stress or life-threatening situations, our sympathetic nervous system kicks in to allow us to think and move quickly. It pulls energy and blood flow from all organs that don't need it at precisely that moment (such as the immune system, the digestive system, and the reproductive system) while at the same time kicking our fight-or-flight apparatus into gear—raising blood pressure, increasing the rate and force of heart contractions, activating sweat secretion, and the like. This is all especially valuable if you are being chased by a bear, though it probably has some value if your boss is screaming at you as well.

The parasympathetic nervous system is the mirror image of the sympathetic nervous system. Its job is to slowly bring everything back to equilibrium after the sympathetic nervous system has put your body on high alert. It sends blood and energy back to those depleted organs, lowers your blood pressure, and brings your breathing back to normal.

One common argument against the always-on world we live in now is that our sympathetic nervous system is getting far too much work and our parasympathetic nervous system can only watch idly while "temporarily nonvital" organs go far too long in a depleted state. Meditation is considered by many to be something of a salve to this condition, as it shuts down the sympathetic, allows the parasympathetic to do its thing, and gives the pleasure centers of the brain some "me time."

For the most part, when one system is up, the other is down. However, there are circumstances when we need to be aroused and calm at the same time, most notably during sexual activity. In this case, our sympathetic nervous system gets our sexual organs functioning in a maximal way, and our parasympathetic nervous system helps ease us toward eventual completion.

This is a truly persuasive case for the value of paradox, one provided to us by Mother Nature herself.

> There is no love without aggression.
>
> —Konrad Lorenz

The safety of heights and the dangers of soft landings

Some paradoxes seem immune to mixing. For example, one would imagine the line between keeping our children safe and exposing them to increased levels of risk to be a clear and uncrossable one.

However, there's an argument to be made that keeping kids *too* safe might be to their detriment in the long run.

In the past few decades, playgrounds have been reengineered to be much safer environments. Considerably lower climbing walls have replaced ten-foot-tall monkey bars, and concrete pavements have given way to rubberized surfaces. The upshot is a decline in concussions and lawsuits, but the rate of injury has not decreased nearly as much as one might expect. The reason for this might very well be that because children think they can't get hurt, they're actually being less careful and learning less about using caution than they would if the equipment seemed more dangerous to them. Where kids once understood that they'd bang themselves up badly if they landed hard on concrete, they underestimate the damage that can be done by falling a few feet onto something that appears soft.

The bigger risk, though, might be from what children are losing by no longer being exposed to more dangerous playgrounds. "Risky play mirrors effective cognitive behavioral therapy of anxiety," said psychologists Ellen Sandseter and Leif Kennair in the journal *Evolutionary Psychology.* "Paradoxically, we posit that our fear of children being harmed by mostly harmless injuries may result in more fearful children and increased levels of psychopathology."

The notion here is that children rarely got seriously injured while playing on the more dangerous playgrounds and that, overall, they benefited from conquering a certain level of risk. The playgrounds of old were a study in the benefits of paradox: They were dangerous, but rarely *really* dangerous; you could simulate danger and experience the feeling of mastering this danger without taking any truly big chances. On the other hand, not learning to conquer these relatively small risks can leave one phobic. Studies have even shown that children who are hurt in a fall before the age of nine are less likely to develop a fear of heights.

For a piece for the *New York Times*, journalist John Tierney visited a playground in Fort Tryon Park in Manhattan that had one of the few ten-foot-high jungle gyms left in the city. While he was there, he asked a ten-year-old girl and her mother what they thought of the apparatus. "I was scared at first," the girl said, "but my mother said if you don't try, you'll never know if you could do it. So I took a chance and kept going. At the top I felt very proud."

"It's kind of dangerous, I know," said the mother, "but if you just think about danger you're never going to get ahead in life."

This is another benefit of paradox: It gives us a sense of parameters. When one explores one thing and its seeming opposite, what you discover at the same time is what lies in between.

This notion of the value of play spaces as a testing ground for one's response and acclimation to danger reminds me of Gregory Bateson's discussion of play in his book *Steps to an Ecology of Mind*. In it, he discusses the connection between the "artificiality" of play and that of therapy.

The resemblance between the process of therapy and the phenomenon of play is, in fact, profound. Both occur within a delimited psychological frame, a spatial and temporal bounding of a set of interactive messages. In both play and therapy, the messages have a special and peculiar relationship to a more concrete or basic reality. Just as the pseudocombat of play is not real combat, so also the pseudolove and pseudohate of therapy are not real love and hate. The "transfer" is discriminated from real love and hate by signals invoking the psychological frame; and indeed it is this frame which permits the transfer to reach its full intensity and to be discussed between patient and therapist.

With this, from a very different perspective, Bateson points to the same paradox that Sandseter and Kennair addressed in their article and Tierney addressed in his. While play and therapy are not "real," in that the participants are replicating rather than engaging in experiences, they give us a chance to prepare for the genuine thing. They are a form of practice that allows us to demystify the experience and therefore be ready to deal with it if we must.

Mother Nature's daughter

What's the most effective platform for a designer to launch a line of animal-rights-friendly clothing? Most would not suggest a partnership with Gucci, whose leather goods are the hallmark of their brand. Yet this is exactly the paradox Stella McCartney used to drive her label to international success.

McCartney has a very famous last name, and her father is famously an animal-rights activist (though admittedly he is much more famous for playing bass in a rock band). Her clothing line would have gotten a considerable level of attention regardless of who distributed it. However, the Gucci connection took the conversation to another level. The paradox created the kind of contrast that allowed McCartney to highlight what she was doing without making the clothing line all about the issue. This is important to her.

"It's my job to make people not notice that I'm working in a slightly more responsible way," she told the *Guardian*. "I am a fashion designer. I'm not an environmentalist. When I get up in the morning, number one I'm a mother and a wife, and number two I design clothes. So the main thing I need to do is create, hopefully, exquisitely beautiful, desirable objects for my customer. That's my job, first and foremost. If I can make you not notice that it happens to be out of biodegradable fake suede, if I can make you not notice that it hasn't killed cows or goats or unborn baby lambs, then I'm doing my job. There should be no compromise for you as a customer. I don't want to do scratchy, oatmeal-colored things; that defeats the object."

Another paradox for McCartney is that, given her convictions, she's chosen to work in a profession that consistently flouts the standards that matter to her so deeply.

"People in fashion just don't want to hear the messages," she said in the same interview. "I find it astounding, because fashion is supposed to be about change—I mean, we're supposed to be at the cutting edge! I can only think they don't care as much as people in other industries. So, yes, I think people in fashion are pretty heartless. . . . They must be! Why on earth would they use fur and leather otherwise? There's no excuse for fur in this day and age. Baby kids are boiled alive. Foxes are anally electrocuted. If that's not heartless, what is?"

A few years back, she distributed a video about the grim nature of the fur trade to others in her field. While some applauded this action, many, such as designer Karl Lagerfeld, criticized her or expressed offense.

The paradox has worked for her in the way that paradox works best—by highlighting what makes something distinctive. By having both an inspired design sensibility and a passion for her cause, Stella McCartney has discovered how to juxtapose two seemingly contrary concepts in a manner that the public has embraced. Her partnership with Gucci has prospered in spite of its contradictions, and today she is one of the world's most recognizable figures in fashion—so much so that there are likely to be fashionistas out there who think of Paul McCartney as the father of the famous clothing designer.

FAP

One of the primary reasons that my clients hire me these days is to help them to better connect a product or service to its audience. In the process of this work, I've developed a strong thesis about popularity that has much to do with paradox. I call this concept "FAP": Familiarity, Appeasement, and Power.

For something to be popular, it first needs to be familiar in some way. The audience needs to be able to say, "It's like me," and to gain a level of comfort from that. One of the things I've come to realize is that familiarity is not about satisfaction; it's about relief. As we discussed earlier in this book, our psyches can't handle new information all the time. Therefore, when we come up against something familiar, we relax, because we don't need to work hard to deal with it. When the online megastore Zappos first entered the market, it took a fresh approach to selling shoes, but it still felt and acted like a store. Therefore, we could at once experience the paradox of trying something new and trying something familiar.

Next, the audience needs to feel a sense of appeasement from the product or service, to be able to say, "It *likes* me." We like to feel that we are a part of something, and things that are popular tend to share affinity with those who engage in it. Before the first iPhone was released in 2007, cell phones tended to be confounding and only marginally effective. The iPhone completely changed the game because it seemed to be saying, "I get you, and I think we can have a lot of fun together." Again, there was a paradox at work. The product flaunted its superiority over the competition that existed at the time while at once acting like "one of the guys" to the consumer.

Finally, the product or service needs to provide the audience with a sense of power. It needs to make you feel that, by using it, you can be more of yourself and accomplish more of what you want to accomplish. Google provides its users with a tremendous sense of power because it affords them with access to a vast amount of information that was either inaccessible or much harder to access before. In so doing, it provides its audience with increased opportunity for self-expansion. The paradox at play here is that by exhibiting its own power, the product or service makes the user feel more powerful.

(For the sake of illustration, I used three different products or services, but it's important to point out that all three of these exhibit all three components of FAP. The iPhone, for instance, shows familiarity in the ease of its interface, even making it possible at this point for a consumer to access many of its functions without pressing buttons. It also provides power by putting a huge portion of the world in the palm of a user's hand.)

The three components of FAP combine to create emotional engagement, and without emotional engagement, the public is unlikely to care about anything for long. And as FAP shows, paradox is at the very center of popularity. In fact, it is nearly impossible to imagine something being popular without a considerable sense of paradox.

The beginning of the and

The most interesting things in our lives come with the word *and* attached to them. Safety and danger. Confidence and doubt. Sincerity and cynicism. Expectation and surprise. When you choose to activate your abilities to mix seemingly unlike things, you open the door to creativity and growth. We can see this in some of our most iconic and enduring celebrities: Brando was tough and tender; Jagger is childlike and devilish; Garbo was chaste and seductive.

But where we really see it is in our own lives. Consider your favorite pursuits and your most unforgettable experiences. Are you engaged in your work because it makes you feel the same way every day, or does it excite you because sometimes it lifts you up *and* sometimes it makes you want to bang your head against the wall? Do you love traveling to other countries because everything is familiar or because some of it is familiar *and* some of it is utterly exotic? Do you cherish your best friends because things are always predictable when you're with them, or is it because they're both comfortable to be with *and* challenging?

It dawned on me recently that virtually every positive review I've ever read of a book, performance, restaurant, or anything else that falls under the critical eye underscores the paradoxes inherent in the work. The critics applaud a filmmaker's ability to be wise and innocent at the same time, a musician's skill at being studied and spontaneous, a dancer's precision and looseness. Critics celebrate paradox for the same reason we all should: because paradox makes us come alive.

Putting your Essential of paradox to work helps you to look at the world in new ways. If you're accustomed to considering something from one perspective, regarding it from the opposite perspective is likely to add nuance and depth to your approach. Paradox helps you to innovate. One of the most effective ways to operate uniquely within a domain is to incorporate something of the opposite into your work. Paradox also helps you to get beyond the habitual. You are considerably less likely to fall into a rut if you regularly alternate between a pursuit and its seeming opposite. And perhaps most significantly, paradox gives "elbow room" to your self-story by expanding your range of possibilities and the parameters of your exploits.

Paradox is not a problem we need to solve. It is an opportunity for us to get real.

chapter five

The Essential of Self-Story

Aᴄᴄᴏʀᴅɪɴɢ ᴛᴏ ʜᴇʀ mother, Debra Byrd "cut her own umbilical cord."

"She said when she gave birth to me, I basically walked away," Byrd told me. "I remember being a kid and my mother used to say things to me like, 'Don't be so driven.' I'd say, 'Sorry, Mom, I just am.' If I'm not driven, I will probably perish."

Byrd is an internationally acclaimed singer and singing mentor, having served as vocal coach for *American Idol* and *Canadian Idol*, performed with Bob Dylan and Barry Manilow, and had roles in five Broadway plays. She believes that she came out of the womb with a strong sense of possibility and that it has carried her throughout her life.

"I'm Shirley Temple—you know, rosy. I look at life through rose-colored glasses, even when I unknowingly worked for a gangster. I'm singing backup for this guy that's got lots of money and I'm just there, oh, it's a wonderful time. One of the backup singers says, 'This is gangster stuff. Don't you realize it?' No, I

didn't realize it. And sure enough, after we did this huge extrav-
aganza, he was in jail. When I was a little girl, I used to look in
the mirror and go, 'Why am I here? What is this about?' I've
come to respect destiny."

More than most people I meet, Byrd has a very strong sense
of who she is and seemed to have a clear picture of where she was
going from an early age. At an innate level, she understood that
her life had a story and that she was not only living it, but leading
it. She knew that music was at the center of that story, but she
had no idea that her talent made her extraordinary.

"I didn't know people couldn't sing. It never dawned on me
because I was always surrounded by people who can sing and
sing very, very well. I never thought I was anything special, never.
I never thought I had anything different from anybody else. But I
do know that I worked my butt off. I worked very hard because I
loved it. But that's what my family background was, so it never,
ever in a million years dawned on me that I was anything special."

As she refined her talent, something else emerged: a clear
sense that music was taking her down a particular path.

"I'm trained to sing opera. I was trained from the time I was
twelve to perform at the Met. I sing in five languages. But having
a rock-and-roll heart . . . 'I'll be right back, opera; I'm going to go
over here and do some rock and roll.' It was literally, 'Okay, I
won't audition for the Met; I'll audition for things that involve
pop music. I'll look for a record deal.' I believe after deciding I'm
not going to sing opera for a living, I decided to listen to what
else is out there. I became about the study of singers and their
styles. I believe that's where I went. Knowing that I had a rock-
and-roll heart is, like, 'Okay, you love what rock is—fine. Do

other things.' With that, I worked on my voice, myself, so that I could make that transition from being this Italian opera diva into singing popular music and knowing the difference between a standard and a classical song or an opera song. I think I began being a music historian."

This sense of being truly aware of where her story was taking her has served Byrd very well. She could have been an accomplished opera singer, but her heart wasn't in it. She could have pursued a major role at the front of the stage, but she understood that her skill as a music historian and as someone who could dissect and improve the performances of others was where her greatest strengths lay. She has carved a distinct place for herself in the world she loves because she never lost focus on her story, never betrayed who she really was. At the same time, she understands better than most that the world might have things in store for all of us that we can't possibly anticipate—but that we can make the most of the opportunities if we know who we are and are watching carefully enough.

"I don't make predictions. I'd be remiss if I tried to make a prediction. All I can do is fasten my seat belt, ride the wave, and pay attention."

From the moment she "cut her own umbilical cord," Debra Byrd has been making full use of the Essential of self-story. She knows who she is, she knows when important decisions feel right, and while she doesn't presume to know exactly where the road is taking her, she has a fairly good idea of where she's going.

The narrative of you

Self-story is the power booster of your internal resource pack. It is the resource for which your other resources work in service, and it is, in my opinion, the most important resource for you to develop.

Simply put, your self-story is what you are *about*. It is you as an idea that stands above the press of the moment. It is the configuration of both the events that define your life and what those events represent. As I mentioned earlier, it isn't your biography or the entries to your diary. Instead, it is the you that rises out of your day-to-day life. It is the essential you. It is the eternal you. It is the you that you are and the you that you can be. When you are fully aware of your self-story, you are capable of being your most authentic self—your most innovative, most valuable, and happiest self.

During his series of conversations with Bill Moyers, broadcast by PBS as *The Power of Myth*, Joseph Campbell referenced an essay from the philosopher Arthur Schopenhauer that comes very close to defining self-story:

> Schopenhauer, in his splendid essay called "On an Apparent Intention in the Fate of the Individual," points out that when you reach an advanced age and look back over your lifetime, it can seem to have had a consistent order and plan, as though composed by some novelist. Events that when they occurred had seemed accidental and of little moment turn out to have been indispensable factors in the composition of a consistent plot. So who composed that

plot? Schopenhauer suggests that just as your dreams are composed by an aspect of yourself of which your consciousness is unaware, so, too, your whole life is composed by the will within you. And just as people whom you will have met apparently by mere chance became leading agents in the structuring of your life, so, too, will you have served unknowingly as an agent, giving meaning to the lives of others. The whole thing gears together like one big symphony, with everything unconsciously structuring everything else.

What Campbell is discussing here is something closely akin to self-story—the notion that our lives have a narrative thread, that we are all in some way like the great literary characters we have been reading, and that we exert a meaningful force on each other's narratives. Looking at our lives in this way raises us above the mundanity of the day-to-day toward something more meaningful, while at the same time making clear to us a path about which we might have otherwise been unaware.

Neuroscientist Antonio Damasio takes this further in his book *The Feeling of What Happens*. "Our traditional notion of self," he says, "is linked to the idea of identity and corresponds to a nontransient collection of unique facts and ways which characterize a person. My term for that entity is the 'autobiographical self.'" What he is identifying for us is that we literally create ourselves through narrative.

Your self-story comes in three parts. One of these, of course, is your sense of who you are as a person. In Debra Byrd's case, she knew very early in her life that she was a musician and that being one defined her at a fundamental level. However, who you are is not always about what you do for a living or even what you like to do. Instead, it could be about a particular trait that guides you ("I'm a kind person." "I'm a charitable person." "I'm a badass."), or about a particular role you fill within your social circle. Someone I know is an extremely successful professional who works long hours and pursues his career with great vigor. When I asked him how he would describe himself, he responded by saying, "I think I'm nice." My first thought was that he was being modest or even a bit disingenuous, but when I gave it more thought, I realized that "nice" was actually a fundamental component of his self-story. He'd built his professional relationships around being approachable, his career around inclusion, and his personal life around helping others. In his case, being nice was a definitive component of his story.

The second part of your self-story is your worldview, your particular perspective on how the universe works. Are you someone who sees signs everywhere? Are you someone who believes that life will work in your favor if you are diligent and passionate enough? Are you someone who thinks the world is out to get you? Are you a "the world is made up of two kinds of people" person? How you see what is happening around you is a critical part of your story. Just as a novelist shades characters with her perceptions of the realm outside her door, all of our stories are colored by our worldview.

When I was in graduate school, I took a class on family dynamics, in which we studied Norman Lear's seminal television comedy *All in the Family*. The show's Archie Bunker had a very clear worldview—he was a bigot. During a classic episode with guest star Sammy Davis Jr., Archie's son-in-law (played by Rob

Reiner before he became a world-class film director) tells Davis's character, "He's not so bad. He wouldn't burn a cross on your lawn." To this, Davis responds, "No, but he might stop to toast a marshmallow." Bunker's worldview—that everyone other than people with his specific background is inferior and dangerous— is a fundamental part of his self-story. It would be impossible to explain what Archie is about without including this. Juxtapose that with Debra Byrd calling herself Shirley Temple to describe her optimistic perspective on the world. While these points of view couldn't be more different, they are in both cases huge components of their respective self-stories.

A third part of your self-story involves what you consider yourself to be a part of and what you think of yourself as apart from. All of us belong to a number of "tribes." These are groups in which we congregate because of professional or social interests. Your tribe might be fellow entrepreneurs, for example, or people who share your passion for bodysurfing. Fellow members of the PTO at your child's school could be a part of your tribe, as might be the commuters you share the same train car with every day. In addition, you might associate yourself with larger communities, centered on the place you live, the kind of entertainment you enjoy, your political party, your religion, your favorite sports team, and more. These things help clarify your self-story. So do the groups that you actively consider yourself not to be a part of. This could be as innocuous as disliking country music or baseball's use of the designated hitter, or something more highly charged like being pro-choice or anti–big government. Where we feel we belong and where we have no interest in belonging tell us a great deal regarding what we're about.

At the same time, it is important to understand what self-story is not. For one thing, it is not a chronicle. Your self-story is not your biography or a listing of your achievements and failings, romances and heartbreaks. It is not important to your self-story that you got a promotion last year or that your first crush snubbed you to go out with the captain of the football team. The point here is that the events themselves do little to contribute to your self-story unless they illustrate something fundamental about you. If the promotion came because of your steadfast belief in giving 110 percent at work or the girl snubbed you because you insisted on wearing a "Disco Sucks" T-shirt three days a week in some vain attempt to seem "edgy," *that* might be meaningful.

The other thing that self-story is not is self-psychoanalysis. You find your self-story by examining the metaphors in your life (more on this in a bit), but not by trying to understand why you've always been shy, had issues with authority, or shunned large crowds. These might be important to who you are, but not to what you're about.

When you examine the three components of self-story, an enduring picture of yourself emerges. This is the narrative you are living, and once you understand what yours is, your life clicks into place in dramatic ways. Having a clear sense of your self-story does two utterly essential things for you at once: It tells you what is true to you, and it tells you what is not true to you. Let's go back to Debra Byrd again. An important piece of her self-story is that she has a "rock-and-roll heart." This helped her to make a decision that led her to a more authentic life. She had the skill to be an opera singer, but if she had taken that path, she would not have been true to her self-story, and in all likelihood she would have been successful but confused about why she wasn't feeling more satisfied. Knowing what you are about helps you to be at the same time very clear regarding what you are *not* about. This allows for the possibility of extraordinary growth, because when a new opportunity comes along, maybe even something you've never considered before, your self-story gives you a way to judge if that opportunity makes sense in your very specific case.

Self-story also makes you resilient in ways that you can't possibly be otherwise. When you truly know what you are about, you know it in an unassailable way. Having a vivid sense of your self-story protects you from being completely thrown off your game in the face of hardship. This doesn't mean that the hardships themselves will be less difficult to endure, but it does mean that you're likely to bounce back from them faster. Consider the small business owners we talked about in chapter two. So many of them define themselves by their businesses, and so many are vulnerable to all kinds of misfortune that rarely befalls someone who makes a living in another way. Those who thrive tend to understand their self-stories—and perhaps more to the point, their business's self-stories—at a cellular level, and because they understand what they are genuinely about, they can get back on their feet more quickly when things trip them up.

> There is a story, always ahead of you. Barely existing. Only gradually do you attach yourself to it and feel it. You discover the carapace that will contain and test your character. You find in this way the path of your life.
>
> —Michael Ondaatje, *The Cat's Table*

Inspired to action

One of the most illuminating components of your self-story is your "creation story." Creation stories are typically associated with cultures or even the totality of humankind. For instance, there's the Scandinavian myth about the birth of the world that involves Odin the All-Father, the terrible Ymir, and the frost giants. Then there's the Cherokee myth of the creation of medicine, which the plants conspired to invent when the animals invented disease in response to being hunted.

However, we all have creation stories, and while ours typically have little to do with huge ogres or deer and bears getting together to stick it to the man, they are a fundamental and illustrative part of our "legend." My own creation story goes all the way back to my birth. I mentioned earlier in this book that I was born almost three months early and had to spend several months in an incubator before I could survive outside the hospital. As a result, I entered the world in extended isolation, a part of it and yet separate from it. I believe that this has contributed to the role I have as an observer. The creation story that I've weaved from these events in my life—events that I couldn't possibly remember, since they happened before I had words—is that the forced remove caused by my beginning life in a box has given me an unusual ability to step back and see things that others miss.

My coauthor, Lou Aronica, has an interesting creation story as well. Two years before he was born, his brother died after an extended illness, throwing his entire family, but especially his mother, into deep grief. A little more than a year later, Lou's mother, who believed she'd already gone through menopause, became pregnant. She immediately declared that God was returning her son and that she would give the child—who she was convinced was a boy, though there were no sonograms to confirm this back then—her deceased son's name. Lou's creation story, then, is that he is living for two people, himself and his late brother.

For Lou and me, our creation stories come in very close proximity to our actual creation. However, your creation story doesn't need to relate to your physical birth. Sometimes it relates to how you emerged into the person you are today. During his South by Southwest keynote, Bruce Springsteen touched on his creation story in several places.

He traced his fascination with rock and roll to seeing Elvis Presley on *The Ed Sullivan Show*. "One week later, inspired by the passion in Elvis's pants," he said during the address, "my little six-year-old fingers wrapped themselves around a guitar neck for the first time. . . . They just wouldn't fit! Failure with a capital *F*! So I just beat on it and beat on it—in front of the mirror, of course. . . . I still do that."

He then pulled his connection back even further. "But even before there was Elvis, my world had begun to be shaped by the little radio with the six-inch mono speaker that sat on top of our refrigerator. My mother loved music, and she raised us on pop music radio. . . . The sounds of early pop whispered itself into my young, impressionable ears.

"In the beginning," he said elsewhere in the speech, "every musician has their genesis moment. For you, it might have been the Sex Pistols, or Madonna, or Public Enemy. It's whatever initially inspires you to action."

With this last sentence, we see a clear path to uncovering our creation stories. It is the thing that "inspires you to action." If you can find the moment or moments when you came face-to-face with something that you knew was going to be very important to you, you've come upon at least a bit of your creation story. And if you have, then your understanding of your self-story has taken a huge leap forward, because where you "began" is maybe the most important part of what you are about.

> Human personal intuition always whispers; it never shouts. Very hard to hear, so you have to every day of your lives be ready to hear what whispers in your ear. If you can listen to the whisper and it tickles your heart and it's something you think you want to do for the rest of your life, then that's going to be what you do for the rest of your life and we will benefit from everything you do.
>
> —Steven Spielberg

Pretty girls and electric eels

Another tremendously valuable way of understanding your self-story is through the prism of metaphor. As Ralph Waldo Emerson explained nearly three centuries ago:

> It is not words only that are emblematic; it is things which are emblematic. Every natural fact is a symbol of some spiritual fact. Every appearance in nature corresponds to some state of the mind, and that state of the mind can only be described by presenting that natural appearance as its

picture. An enraged man is a lion, a cunning man is a fox, a firm man is a rock, a learned man is a torch. A lamb is innocence; a snake is subtle spite; flowers express to us the delicate affections. Light and darkness are our familiar expression for knowledge and ignorance; and heat for love. Visible distance behind and before us, is respectively our image of memory and hope. . . . The world is emblematic. Parts of speech are metaphors, because the whole of nature is a metaphor of the human mind.

Metaphors are wonderfully supple and effective devices. They allow us to replace something we don't yet understand with something we understand well, and in so doing, wrap our minds around the new construct. When asked to explain his theory of relativity to the average person, Albert Einstein turned to metaphor: "Put your hand on a hot stove for a minute, and it seems like an hour. Sit with a pretty girl for an hour, and it seems like a minute. *That's* relativity." Metaphors can convey a huge amount of information in a few words, such as when someone describes going through a particularly rough patch by saying, "I'm having a bear of a week." And they can enhance our appreciation for something we already know by allowing us to see these familiar things in new ways. Keith Richards, of the Rolling Stones, for example, described his instrument of choice this way: "An electric guitar will jump live in your hands. It's like holding on to an electric eel."

In all three of these ways, metaphor is tremendously effective at helping you touch down on your self-story. It can add clarity to your most complex personal circumstances ("My father and I were always tropical storm and straw hut"). It can cover a great deal of ground very quickly ("My twenties were one long green light"). And it can add color to your perspective on events ("My wife flicked the 'on' switch to my heart"). Therefore, if we think of our self-stories from the perspective of metaphor, and if we look for the prevalent metaphors in our lives, we're likely to come away with a richness of understanding about ourselves that we would not otherwise have and a sturdier perspective on what we're about.

Metaphors offer our self-stories one more tremendously vital thing: a way of imbuing in ourselves a sense of the epic. This reflects back on what Campbell and Damasio said earlier in the chapter. Thinking of the overarching symbols of our lives puts those lives on a different scale. Things that seem mundane in the day-to-day take on a different cast when perceived as "platform building" or "a long climb out of the hole" (or, I suppose, "the slow descent into the hole" if things turned out that way). The same is true of years of struggle, a series of bad romantic relationships, or even your wunderkind days in elementary school.

Just as our self-stories help define us, metaphors help define our self-stories.

> Examine all things intensely and relentlessly.
> Probe and search each object in a piece of art.
> Do not leave it, do not course over it, as if it were
> understood, but instead follow it down until you
> see it in the mystery of its own specificity and
> strength.
>
> —Annie Dillard, *The Writing Life*

Our essence, distilled

One of the recurrent themes of this book has been that there is much to be learned from the lessons fictional characters and their creators teach us. In thinking about self-story, I find myself coming back to that theme. As we've noted, our lives, when examined carefully, take on the dimensions, nuance, and resonance of literature. All of our lives have stretches filled with the rising and falling action of a well-plotted story. They all have crystalline moments that divide one's existence into before and after—the birth of a child, perhaps, or the discovery of a passion, or the tragic end of a friendship. They all have, hidden under the mundanity of everyday existence, moments when they touch the mythic, when what we are doing extends beyond ourselves into something universal.

The best fiction writers capture the core of that. Our most enduring novels and short stories live in our hearts because they distill our essences. If we think of our self-stories as ourselves as works of literature, we gain not only a greater sense of our own nobility but also a model for seeking these stories. For more than sixty years now, *The Paris Review* has been running a series of interviews with important writers under the banner "The Art of Fiction." In these interviews, writers from Ralph Ellison to Norman Mailer to Joan Didion to Ray Bradbury discuss their inspirations and their missions. As would be expected from a diverse group of more than two hundred writers, the conversations go in a large number of directions. One topic that comes up often, however, is one that seems particularly relevant to self-story: that no event or image is too small to have profound implications.

For example, William Faulkner, in response to a question about how his novel *The Sound and the Fury* began, responded:

> It began with a mental picture. I didn't realize at the time it was symbolical. The picture was of the muddy seat of a little girl's drawers in a pear tree, where she could see through a window where her grandmother's funeral was taking place and report what was happening to her brothers on the ground below. By the time I explained who they were and what they were doing and how her pants got muddy, I realized it would be impossible to get all of it into a short story and that it would have to be a book. And then I realized the symbolism of the soiled pants, and that image was replaced by the one of the fatherless and motherless girl climbing down the drainpipe to escape from the only home she had, where she had never been offered love or affection or understanding.

Here, Don DeLillo talks about the image that vaulted his novel *Americana* to life:

> I don't always know when or where an idea first hits the nervous system, but I remember *Americana*. I was sailing in Maine with two friends, and we put into a small harbor on Mt. Desert Island. And I was sitting on a railroad tie waiting to take a shower, and I had a glimpse of a street maybe fifty yards away and a sense of beautiful old houses and rows of elms and maples and a stillness and wistfulness—the street seemed to carry its own built-in longing. And I felt something, a pause, something opening up before me. It would be

a month or two before I started writing the book and two or three years before I came up with the title *Americana*, but in fact it was all implicit in that moment—a moment in which nothing happened, nothing ostensibly changed, a moment in which I didn't see anything I hadn't seen before. But there was a pause in time, and I knew I had to write about a man who comes to a street like this or lives on a street like this. And whatever roads the novel eventually followed, I believe I maintained the idea of that quiet street if only as counterpoint, as lost innocence.

In her *Paris Review* interview, Margaret Drabble addresses the little things from a different perspective:

What I'm perpetually trying to work out is the relationship between coincidence and plan. And in fact, I have this deep conviction that if you were to get high up enough over the world, you would see things that look like coincidence are, in fact, part of a pattern. This sounds very mystical and ridiculous, but I don't think it is. I think that I, in particular, and maybe certain other people, have a need to perceive this pattern in coincidence. It may be that psychologically we're so afraid of the unpredictable, of the idea of chaos and disorder, that we wish to see order.

Take the fact that you should bump into somebody after ten years on your birthday after having last seen them at your birthday party. This is a coincidence, but it appears to have a meaning. We know it's superstitious, but so many times in my life I've had coincidences like this that I'm driven to look for another underlying meaning.

What each of these writers is addressing in the realm of fiction *works* in the realm of fiction because it reflects so strongly on our real lives. If we're truly paying attention, how many times do mental snapshots or seeming coincidences say something powerful about who we are and what we're about? When you consider your childhood, do you tend to go back to a day on a playground when nothing in particular happened? Does a chance meeting on the street stick with you for years after it occurred? Do you for some reason remember what you or someone else was wearing on an otherwise ordinary day? There might be something at work there that speaks to your self-story, and it is certainly worth examining in this context.

The alchemy of limitations

There's also much to be learned about your self-story in considering your limitations. A few years ago, after hearing one of his favorite piano concertos played in a way that left him unmoved, Daniel Levitin, professor and James McGill Chair in psychology, in the Department of Psychology at McGill University, began a study into the emotional effect of musical performance. He had several pieces recorded digitally by a pianist using a special keyboard, and then altered that performance to set a baseline for the pieces precisely as the composer had written them, without any variation from the performer. He and his assistants then created several alternative versions with variations on the volume, speed, and intensity with which the notes were played. They then played the various pieces for study subjects, who overwhelmingly found the original performance—the one in which the pianist added his own style and his own "errors" into the music—to be the one that moved them the most. What was obvious was that these flaws were what gave the work its immediacy and richness.

In discussing this experiment, singer Rosanne Cash makes the point that the human component, and all the imperfections that humans bring to an endeavor, is what makes music resonate with listeners. Her father, the great country star Johnny Cash, instilled in her the notion that "your style is a function of your limitations, more so than a function of your skills."

"You've heard plenty of great, great singers that leave you cold," she says. "They can do gymnastics, amazing things. If you have limitations as a singer, maybe you're forced to find nuance in a way you don't have to if you have a four-octave range."

The point that Cash is making here is that our very limitations are what make us most interesting. When trying to perform a task despite lacking the innate skills to accomplish it easily, we invent our own way of doing it—and this can very well have a more meaningful effect than if we've done everything perfectly. When I think of making the most of one's talent in spite of limitations, I think of baseball player Pete Rose. Rose (whose oft-reported character flaws go beyond the scope of this particular conversation) was rarely the player on the field with the greatest physical gifts. He wasn't particularly fast, and he wasn't particularly powerful, at least in terms of his ability to hit home runs. These limitations led him to have trouble even making his high school varsity baseball team. Yet he eventually became enormously effective because he simply seemed to try harder than everyone else on the field, a trait that earned him the nickname Charlie Hustle. Ultimately, he wound up with the most hits and the twenty-seventh best offensive production statistics in the history of baseball, because he found ways to do things that he might not have discovered if he'd had a greater amount of natural talent.

Nobuyuki Tsujii is the first blind pianist to win the Van Cliburn International Piano Competition. Tsujii has perfect pitch, something that is extremely common in those who are born blind. Neurologist and best-selling author Oliver Sacks, who has studied the connection between music and the brain extensively, believes that as many as half of those born blind have this asset naturally.

However, Tsujii has employed his combination of blindness and perfect pitch to create a style that is uniquely his. Rather than relying on Braille music, which is relatively readily available, Tsujii learns to play everything, including extremely complex concertos, by memorizing the way it sounds. He asks assistants to record the left hand of a piece in small sections on one recording and the right hand on another, also asking them to avoid interpreting the music in any way (he would obviously benefit from Daniel Levitin's team of researchers). It can take him a month or more to memorize the recordings and to combine his two hands, but when he does, it emerges as something uniquely his. In large part, this is because he doesn't have access to sheet music. He doesn't perform the music as the composer intended it to be played. Instead, he performs it as he feels it should be played.

The result is that a Nobuyuki Tsujii piano performance is like no other. Said *Boston Globe* music critic Richard Dyer after serving as a judge during Tsujii's Van Cliburn competition, "Very seldom do I close my notebook and just give myself over to it, and he made that necessary. I didn't want to be interrupted in what I was hearing." Menahem Pressler, another Cliburn juror, said, "God has taken his eyes, but given him the physical endowment and mental endowment to encompass the greatest works of piano. . . . I had to keep from crying when I listened." Van Cliburn himself even said, "You feel God's presence in the room when he plays. His soul is so pure, his music is so wonderful and it goes to infinity, to the highest heaven."

There is the very real chance that Nobuyuki Tsujii would have been a great pianist even if he had his sight. However, the way he has dealt with his limitations has made him a truly distinctive pianist. This shows what he is about in a way that his blindness never could.

Danny DeVito is a world-renowned actor known for leading roles in the television shows *Taxi* and *It's Always Sunny in Philadelphia* and films like *Batman Returns* and *Throw Momma from the Train*. At five feet tall and round, he has had to counter expectations his entire career in order to get roles that didn't focus exclusively on his height or body type. He has used his stature—and the dynamics created from playing against type—to his benefit.

"Early on," he told an interviewer, "when I'd go in for a part, people would go, 'Oh.' Later, when they rewind that meeting, it would be, 'We've seen twenty actors for the role of the servant in *The Merry Wives of Windsor*, but wait a minute, we've done this already with this guy, so let's try this Danny guy.' I got two Shakespeare parts like that."

One could easily see DeVito's height as a disadvantage or

limitation. Other than Peter Dinklage, an actor who has starred in a wide variety of roles despite being less than five feet tall, it's difficult to think of many men in this field who have been able to thrive while being so short. However, DeVito exudes presence, something that might not be nearly as noticeable if he were even six or seven inches taller. While the contrast between his appearance and his persona comes across first because one wouldn't naturally assume such intensity from someone who looks like DeVito, it lingers because of his impressive technique. Like the singer without the four-octave range or the ballplayer without extraordinary speed or power, DeVito has had to build outward from his limitations to create a unique place for himself—and in the process identify a self-story that is exclusively his.

> Know your own bone; gnaw at it, bury it, unearth
> it, and gnaw it still.
>
> —Henry David Thoreau

Listening to "the Interpreter"

Why is awareness of your self-story so valuable? Because it offers you the clearest path toward self-actualization. If a life well lived is one that involves meaning and a sense of accomplishment, your self-story is the Essential that works in the service of providing that life.

As human beings, we are always seeking a narrative. Cognitive neuroscientist Michael Gazzaniga substantiated this for us in an extensive study of split-brain patients, people who'd had the connection cut between their left and right hemispheres. This work allowed him to study the two hemispheres independent of each other. "Over many, many years," he said in an interview with Big Think, "the basic finding is that one brain didn't know what the other was doing. The information doesn't transfer between the brains. We found out that in the left brain, there's a special system that seems to always want to explain actions and moods that we had after they occurred. We would put a question to the right, nonspeaking hemisphere, and it would, in effect, direct the left hand to do something. Then we would say to the patient, 'Why did you do that?' The patient would make up a story that would explain why their hand had done one thing and why the other hand had done another thing, and wove a tale that made coherent, as it were, the behaviors that are coming from all these separate brain areas. The behavior comes out and then there's this little narrator that turns it into a story that makes it feel coherent and unified.

"It turns out there's a thing in the left hemisphere that does this. We called it 'the Interpreter.' It's a very powerful force in the human condition and it's always trying to figure out and seek explanations for our behavior."

He goes on in the interview to discuss the role of fiction in our lives. "I think the human is a storytelling animal, as some people put it, because this system is continually trying to keep the story coherent. Why does the human always seem to like fiction? Could it be, as some people have suggested, that it prepares us for unexpected things that happen in our life, because we've already thought about them in our fantasy world or read about them in a fictitious setting and saw how those characters acted, and so when we're confronted with it, we're ready? We've sort of lived through that movie, as it were."

Creating narrative is a fundamental part of our existence. Stories provoke our memory and give us the framework for much of our understanding. As Gazzaniga has shown us, our brains are built to coalesce seemingly random events. If the Interpreter is such a crucial contributor to our thinking, doesn't it then behoove us to have the clearest possible understanding of the narrative we're creating? Simply understanding what we're about makes us more comfortable in our own skin and imbues us with a sense of mission, of living our stories.

But of course our self-stories provide more than that. Our self-stories propel us. Once you have a sense of who you are as an idea, it is then possible for you to build a commitment to that idea. You can move confidently forward toward the embellishment of that idea, embracing behaviors that reinforce it and rejecting those that detract from it. This allows us to live authentically, to make decisions in context, and to keep from doing things that run counter to our stories.

In some ways, this might feel confining. You might say, "What if I don't want to stay in the same box for my entire life?" I'll answer that by saying that if your story feels like a box of any type, it probably isn't really your story. What we're about doesn't stop evolving until we die. Our stories are organic; they are always growing and changing as we grow and change. As we've discussed in these pages, our stories have a shape, but that shape isn't closed on all sides. At least one side is always open to allow us to expand. However, that expansion is much less chaotic and much more productive when we allow it to be guided by an awareness of the narrative we've been living. This is why it is so utterly important that you make the best possible use of this resource. Your self-story allows you to be who you are supposed to be, especially when you utilize five fundamental processes that allow you to make the best use of your Essentials in the service of your self-story.

You'll see these in action in the second portion of this book.

part 2

THE FIVE KEY
PROCESSES

chapter six

Always Be on Your Way Home

CHUCK JONES was the multi-award-winning animator responsible for some of the most enduring cartoon creations of all time—the Road Runner, Wile E. Coyote, Pepé Le Pew, and the definitive versions of Bugs Bunny and Daffy Duck, among others. Seemingly from a very early age, he was moving toward a path for his life that was uniquely his.

"When I was two years old," he said in the documentary *Chuck Jones: Memories of Childhood*, "something that occurred then probably had a great deal to do with my becoming an animator. I fell off of a second-story back porch onto a hunk of cement. I'm sure that it jostled my brain cells out of any hope that I would be a logical child." Whether that was the case or not, Jones saw the world from a distinctive perspective. One of his earliest memories was of standing on the beach and convincing himself that he could orchestrate the movements of the ocean, the scurrying of birds along the sand, and the path of geese flying overhead to coordinate with the soundtrack playing in his head.

Evidence of this signature connection between imagination and nature shows up in so much of his work.

So does a sense of wonder born from moving to Hollywood when he was very young and living in a world in which the lines between fantasy and reality were so completely blurred.

"It never occurred to me that every little boy in the world could not come out of his front porch and see Mary Pickford ride by on a white horse. . . . Our house on Sunset Boulevard was only two blocks from the Chaplin Studio, so we could go down there and press our noses against the fence."

Juxtaposed with this was the dichotomy of his home life. His mother "felt that children could do no wrong" and supported his every effort. When Jones began to show a passion for drawing at an early age, she seemed to know instinctively that she should never suggest to him that she couldn't identify what he was drawing, since doing so might have caused him to question his talents. The unalloyed love he received from his mother stood in stark contrast to the treatment he got from his father. "Father didn't spend a lot of time in our house, which was good for us," Jones said. "He criticized us terribly. He used to beat the hell out of me. He worked me over pretty bad. I remember once displaying that I had black and blue marks all the way from my heels to the back of my neck from him whipping me."

In spite of this, Jones's father managed to provide two valuable services other than staying out of the way. The first involved his failing in a series of entrepreneurial attempts. During each, the elder Jones would print new stationery on fine bond paper and order a supply of pencils with the company name imprinted on them. When the enterprises went under, as they always did, the children would be given the supplies and told to use them up. The three Jones kids would accomplish this by drawing endlessly.

The other thing that Jones's father did was pull Chuck out of his traditional high school to enroll him in Chouinard Art Institute. Jones knew that his father was doing this because he was giving up on his son's ever becoming an accomplished student, but that didn't matter. At Chouinard, Jones found the training he needed to become an animator, even though he had no idea what an animator was when he entered the program.

Once out of school, Jones found a job washing animation cels (the acetate sheets upon which cartoons were once drawn) so they could be reused. This was his first tentative step into the film industry. Soon after, he took a much bigger one, getting a drawing gig with Tex Avery's animation unit at Leon Schlesinger Studios (which would ultimately become the animation division of Warner Bros.). Schlesinger produced Looney Tunes and Merrie Melodies cartoons, and as Jones began to work on these projects, he circled back to the influences of his childhood, including his experiences with a household cat named Johnson. Johnson had an outsize personality that included walking like a bulldog, wearing hollowed-out grapefruit halves on his head, and terrorizing swimmers in the ocean. Echoes of Johnson would appear in Jones's work for more than six decades.

That work ultimately produced three Academy Awards, a star on the Hollywood Walk of Fame, and honorary life membership in the Directors Guild of America. Chuck Jones was so honored because he created a series of characters that both entertained and endeared. Even those he didn't create, like Bugs and Daffy, became the unforgettable figures they are at his hand.

All of these characters came from who Chuck Jones truly was. "Each character represented a trait that resides in me," he said.

For Chuck Jones, the work that defined him was itself defined by a quest to connect with his self-story that began with a fall from a second-story porch. His life followed the path that it did because Jones seemingly had a well-established sense of where his "home" was, he set a course that led him in that direction, and he stayed on that course for the rest of his days.

> I believe that the fundamental experiences of your life form crystals in your imagination, and that you can take your imagination and beam it through from different angles. It hits the crystal, you beam it through this way, you beam it through on another angle, and you end up with different stories, different aperçus, different novels.
>
> —Norman Mailer

Three steps in the right direction

The first part of this book presented you with the five resources that are resident inside you, four of which contribute to the fifth, supreme resource, self-story. Now we're going to walk through five processes that will help you make the most of your self-story. Each involves the integration of all the other resources in particular ways, and all will help you move your life in a direction that is truer to who you really are.

The first of these processes is Always Be on Your Way Home. This means you should be on a continuous quest to be who you were meant to be, that you should set yourself on a path that leads increasingly toward authenticity rather than away from it. One of the things I find fascinating about the Chuck Jones story is that his actions suggest that he always owned up to who he was. He knew he wasn't "logical," he was fascinated and influenced by things that surprised him, and he had a rare talent as an animator. He didn't try to fit himself into someone else's box or tamp down his eccentricities to play it safe. Instead, he let his imagination run wild. By all indications, he knew that "home" for him was a place where sarcastic rabbits got the better of everyone, where coyotes never caught their prey—regardless of how many devices they ordered from the Acme company—and where a dot and a line could fall in love. I have no way of knowing for sure if Chuck Jones felt fulfilled (though when he was in his late eighties he was quoted as saying, "I have unbridled enthusiasm and I'm very fortunate. I can't wish anybody better than to be alive"), but I'm guessing from the way he carved out a unique place for himself and thrived on invention that he felt fairly good about who he was.

Chuck Jones was a gigantically gifted man, one of the most talented ever to grace his profession. That isn't the point, and that isn't why I'm using him as an example here. Chuck Jones was *real*, and that had very little to do with his talent and a huge amount to do with his ability to continuously be on his way home.

This process is accessible to all of us, and it involves three steps. The first is to figure out where home is. There are countless tests and quizzes you can take to tell you what you're meant to do with your life. To be honest, though, I don't believe in any of them. I'm sure they get things right some of the time, but I don't think anything as intensely personal as home can be sussed out by answering a series of standardized questions. Instead, maybe there's something to be learned from a simple Italian peasant dish.

I lived for several years in Tuscany. Eating is a very important thing to do there, and I happen to be very good at it, so I fit right in. Visiting friends' houses or any of the dozens of restaurants in our neighborhood, I found myself regularly tucking into a bowl of pappa al pomodoro, the classic Tuscan tomato-bread soup. It seemed that everywhere I went, they were serving pappa al pomodoro, and since it was delicious, I never complained. Soon, I came to realize that, though I was eating this dish regularly, I wasn't eating the *same* dish every time. Each preparation had subtle differences. One restaurant might leave little chunks of bread in the bowl, while the restaurant down the street would incorporate the bread into the soup completely. One friend might top the dish with ricotta, while another added just a sprinkling of fresh basil. It was the same dish, always recognizable as pappa al pomodoro, but every iteration had a delightful differentiation. Those differentiations were defined by what felt right to the person cooking the meal. Each particular presentation of pappa al pomodoro was an evocation of home for the cook.

Many of the people who made this soup for me had been doing so for years. They'd tested variations until they came to an approach that seemed ideal to them. This is precisely what finding home is about. What are you doing when you feel most right?

When have you felt most connected to your life? What variations to your recipe make your experience most delicious? If you haven't been noticing this, start doing it now. This recipe is your recipe for home.

The next step involves figuring out how to get there. Just as there is no one-size-fits-all way to describe how to identify where home is, there is no universal road map to take you there. The identification of home will help you figure it out, though.

Several years ago, a friend of mine was preparing for his wedding. As part of the process, he and his fiancée worked to prepare their vows with the woman who was going to officiate the wedding. Upon reading the vows my friend had written, in which he spoke eloquently about his love for his future wife and his appreciation of the effect she had on him, the woman said to him, "Wow, I hope someday someone writes something like that for me."

A light went off for my friend at that moment. He'd written the vows from his heart, but he'd managed to move a person who'd read countless heartfelt proclamations over the years. It dawned on him then that he might have more of a talent for touching people with his words than he'd ever imagined. He also realized that writing prose that touched people's hearts was an ambition that felt very right to him, though one he'd rarely allowed himself to consider when he was younger. In that revelation, he figured out where home was, coincidentally at a time when he was about to create a new home with the woman he loved. Once he understood this, he set out to put himself in an environment where he could spend more time writing—specifically, writing from the heart—and less time doing the things that didn't fulfill him nearly as much. He saw the signpost for home and he headed in that direction.

Obviously, there are two levels of work here. The first is in identifying the thing that might send you toward home. The second is in changing your conditions so you can get on your way. This work is intensely personal and will be different for every person who does it, but let me illustrate it for you by walking you through how it worked for my friend. The first part was very much akin to a light going off. He discovered that after writing that piece he felt particularly jazzed by the experience. This ratcheted up to another level when he got the response that he did from the person who was officiating the wedding. After that, he kept thinking about both of those experiences. His feelings—his effective use of his Essential of sensuality—told him that there was a message here. Feeling this good about his writing said something profound to him about who he was meant to be, and he wanted to keep this feeling alive.

The rest required a commitment to creating the conditions under which he could explore the possibility of making writing a bigger part of his life. He certainly couldn't quit his job, and it was hardly as though he could find open positions for writers in the classifieds. He realized that the only way he could discover if there was a future for him in this realm was by getting up earlier and spending a couple of hours every morning working on a manuscript. Interestingly, this didn't make him feel more tired. As it turned out, those early-morning sessions energized him for the entire day. To him, this was yet another indication that he was on his way home. In the end, it took him most of a year to finish his first manuscript, but it ultimately allowed him to make a significant course correction in his life. He sold the novel to a publisher and has sold several others since.

Obviously, this story is specific to this person, but the mechanics are similar for everyone: Pay attention when an experience makes you feel your best, and then make some sacrifices. My friend was okay with giving up sleep. That might not work for you. But something will.

You'll discover your own signposts when you identify what home is for you. The first thing to ask yourself when you get to that stage is, "Am I headed home now?" Like my friend, there's a good chance that at this moment you aren't. But also like him, there's the very real chance that you can point yourself in that direction with only a few adjustments. What changes do you need to make to connect with the real you? How much effort is required? How willing are you to put in that effort? The answers will set you off in the direction you need to go.

The third step involves understanding the point of this process. Keep in mind that the name is Always Be on Your Way Home; it isn't Get Home. The goal here isn't to rush toward a destination, after which you look around and say, "What happens now?" The goal is to try to move toward authenticity every day. If you're really on your way home, you'll never get there— and that's great news. Life is never more exciting than when you're doing something that you love to do *and* you're discovering new things while you're doing it.

I think there's an interesting model for this among athletes who find satisfying ways to continue to compete when their playing careers are over. Jerry West comes to mind. West was a guard for the Los Angeles Lakers and enjoyed a storied playing career, including winning an NBA championship, being inducted into the Basketball Hall of Fame, and being named one of the 50 Greatest Players in NBA History. West took his last professional jump shot in 1974, but that hardly meant that he'd arrived home.

Competing in basketball was clearly home to Jerry West, and he continued toward that destination once he'd hung up his sneakers. First, he served as the Lakers' coach for three seasons, getting his team into the playoffs each year. Then he was the team's general manager during one of the most accomplished runs in the history of sports, winning seven championships in twenty years. He left the Lakers in 2002 to become the general manager of the Memphis Grizzlies, and in 2011, at age seventy-three—thirty-seven years after his last game as a player—West joined the executive board of the Golden State Warriors.

Jerry West found home on a basketball court, and he figured out how to get home by working to become one of the best ever to play the game. Equally important, though, he seemed to understand that he never needed to arrive home; he only needed to continue to be on his way there. This step in the process is critical for all of us. Always being on your way home is about constantly digging deeper to discover the nuances and unmined pleasures in the things you love. It isn't about getting your number retired and spending the rest of your life on your golf game. It's about continually finding new ways to participate in your most fulfilling experiences.

> We live in linear time—we have no choice—but the
> curve of our memory is never a straight line.
>
> —Jeanette Winterson

Making a home by breaking with tradition

As I mentioned earlier in the chapter, all the processes we're going to discuss in the second portion of this book are achieved by
using each of the four other Essentials toward a specific goal, with
the ultimate object being the enhancement of your self-story.

The Essential of curiosity is critical to the process of Always
Be on Your Way Home, because only if you are curious enough
can you discover the signposts that lead you where you need to
go. The story of my writer friend suggests that the inspiration to
pursue this profession came with a sudden revelation. However,
it only functioned that way because of my friend's curiosity. If
he'd written the vows, accepted the compliment graciously, and
then moved on to which Beatles song they should play at the
wedding ceremony, he might be headed anywhere but home
these days. Instead, he was curious enough about the feelings the
experience evoked that he decided to explore further.

Curiosity offers something else in the service of this process:
freedom. When you're curious, you allow yourself the freedom
to look beyond the borders of your current existence. Curiosity
permits you to understand that you might not be terribly close to
home right now and lets you explore both the location of home
and the journey you need to take to get there.

One of the ways in which this manifests itself is with breaking people out of traditional roles. There's a great deal to celebrate
about tradition, including a sense of belonging and an "operating
system" that makes it easier for one to navigate through the world.
However, tradition can be restraining. For example, for more
than a century now, the children of American immigrants have

found that they need to extend beyond the bounds of their old-world traditions if they are to make an authentic place for themselves.

There are also strong traditions related to gender. Even in twenty-first-century America, many roles are still seen as traditionally male or traditionally female. The Missouri Center for Career Education sought to address this by creating the Breaking Traditions awards in 2007. As their website states, these awards are given to "those studying for careers that are traditionally chosen by the opposite gender." In order to qualify, a Missouri student must be involved in a career-technical program in which seventy-five percent of the student population is from the opposite gender. The winners of 2012 awards included Alyssa Webb, the Secondary Female Award winner, who was one of only five female cadets in the Missouri Cadet Patrol Academy program and who won both the academic and physical fitness awards for her entire class. Michael Lundy, the Postsecondary/Adult Male Award winner, turned to nursing after experiencing the losses to illness of several close family members, including his first wife. He decided that nursing was where he should be because he felt the need to ease people back to health or to help them to manage their suffering. The Postsecondary/Adult Female Award went to Brittany Marshall, who is excelling in the traditionally male study of commercial turf and grounds management and who found fulfilling work as a groundskeeper for a minor-league baseball field.

In each of these cases, curiosity drove these people to discover home in a place where someone of their gender traditionally doesn't find it. This can be meaningful to you even if you don't feel constrained by tradition in any way. What's meaningful is the process these people engaged in, which began with fascination for what might be visible beyond the horizon. If you're looking for home, there's a chance that you might be able to locate it there.

Home is everywhere in the world

Openness offers a vital ingredient to Always Be on Your Way Home: the opportunity for enriched discovery and greater depth to your journey. Openness is important if you are still trying to figure out where home is, because when you are open to the wide variety of input that surrounds you, you stand a much better chance of finding where you're meant to go. It is equally important if you've already discovered home, because it can take you down a road you might have otherwise missed.

Consider television journalist Steve Hartman. Hartman seemed to have found the direction home at the launch of his career, first as a feature reporter and then as a correspondent for several CBS newsmagazine shows. However, his career took a considerable upswing and he hit his stride as a journalist when his openness led him to start a feature series that was itself openness in practice. The series was called "Everybody Has a Story" and involved Hartman throwing a dart at a map of America, visiting the town on which the dart landed, finding a local phone book and choosing a number at random, and interviewing someone who lived in that home. The series generated tremendously positive viewer response, because it underscored the nobility of everyday life. It was also clear that this was Hartman doing exactly what he should be doing. As viewers quickly realized, he was a natural at this, and his enthusiasm for the project was contagious both to participants and to his audience.

In 2010, Hartman took the exercise to the next level with "Everybody in the World Has a Story." Partnering with NASA, he teamed up with Jeff Williams, an astronaut working on the International Space Station. While in zero gravity, Williams would spin an inflatable globe and then point to a random location on that globe, after which Hartman would do what he'd been doing in American locations. The project took Hartman to the Australian Outback (no phone books there), to Córdoba, Argentina (plenty of phones there, along with an inspiring self-made man), to Oman, to Latvia, to India, and elsewhere.

"Why am I traveling around the world to random locations to meet equally random strangers?" Hartman said on his blog in September 2010. "There are a couple answers. First of all, experience has taught me the best way to find fascinating stories is not to look for them. It seems like whenever I leave my assignments to chance, fate hands me a story I would have never dreamed of telling otherwise. And even if I did dream it, I would have never had a clue where to find it. . . . But there's also a greater purpose to this project. I think, as Americans, we live in relative isolation—both literally and figuratively. Most of us don't know a whole lot about the people in other countries, me included.

"We may know their history and politics, but what about their fundamental passions and priorities? We may know a country's leader, but what about its regular citizens—the people you would meet if, hypothetically, you took a few random stabs in the phone book and called them up for coffee? How would their stories compare to ours?"

"Everybody Has a Story" has won Hartman much acclaim and multiple awards. It has also shown him that, for him, home is the road. As I write this, Hartman has inherited the "On the Road" segment from the late Charles Kuralt, and his reports from somewhere in America appear every Friday on the *CBS Evening News*.

How Steve Hartman has found home is a case of directed serendipity in action and a powerful testament to the contribution openness makes to this process. It is, of course, available to all of us.

A symphony for the senses

The Essential of sensuality is important to this process because it literally gives us a "feel" for what is right for us and what is not. As we discussed earlier in this chapter, sensuality can put you or keep you on the path toward home by offering cues that you can pick up if you're paying attention. How often have you gotten a queasy sensation in your gut when you're doing something that doesn't fit what you're about? When you're in a new situation that leaves you a bit disoriented, it's possible that this means you're excited about a vista-opening opportunity. However, it might also mean that this is a situation you shouldn't be in.

Sensuality can also offer you your first steps on the road home. When we make active use of our senses, we find ourselves transforming our world in ways that are both surprising and authentic to us. This is what happened with John D. Boswell.

Boswell is particularly passionate about science. He also has a highly developed ear for music, one that has allowed him to hear something that seemingly no one before him has noticed: that the great science communicators have *melodies* in their voices when they talk about their favorite topics.

Using Auto-Tune software, which allows vocal sounds to be manipulated, Boswell combined an original musical composition with video clips and the "singing" of Carl Sagan and Stephen Hawking to create "A Glorious Dawn," a song about the wonders science offers us. He released the video on YouTube and it has generated more than eight million views to date. He has created fourteen additional videos so far, covering topics such as our place in the cosmos, the value of colonizing Mars, the big bang, the lives of dinosaurs, and others. "Lead vocalists" include Richard Feynman, Jane Goodall, Michio Kaku, Bill Nye, Alice Roberts, and Neil deGrasse Tyson.

"The goal of the project," Boswell says on the Symphony of Science website, "is to bring scientific knowledge and philosophy to the public, in a novel way, through the medium of music. Science and music are two passions of mine that I aim to combine, in a way that is intended to bring a meaningful message to listeners, while simultaneously providing an enjoyable musical experience."

While Boswell is involved in a variety of projects, it's clear from the regular posts on the Symphony of Science Facebook page that this particular undertaking has brought him toward home. By turning his senses to the world and by hearing something that others do not, he has been able to do something that is uniquely him.

Your senses can offer the same to you. What do you hear that gets your heart beating faster? What particular things resonate deep inside you when you see them? What do you touch, smell, and taste that makes you feel most motivated? What can you do about this? The answers to these questions can point you home.

A very strange map of home

As we've discussed elsewhere, paradox is the juxtaposition of seemingly unlike things to reveal something new to us. That new thing might very well be home.

Frank Jacobs has found a unique place in the blogosphere by following maps. However, the maps he follows aren't going to be putting Garmin or Rand McNally out of business. He identified a fascinating paradox—that maps can show us the way even when they're out of proportion, inaccurate, or completely invented—and has been writing about it since 2006.

"When photography replaced painting as the main way of depicting reality," Jacobs told an interviewer, "that's when painters really took off in strange directions. Surrealism, symbolism, impressionism, and expressionism were born because artists were liberated from the need to depict reality. Maybe the same thing is happening in cartography."

The first map Jacobs posted on his blog *Strange Maps* showed the location of insane asylums in Pennsylvania. "It provided a bizarre geography of insanity," he said, "and it interested me because it was not the kind of map that would have a place in mainstream cartography. Equally, the map didn't tell us much about mental health. I loved it because it was such an interesting juxta-position of a condition that is so difficult to define with something as cool, rational, and delineated as cartography."

The same could be said of a moral map drawn during Prohibition; a map with the continents of Europe, Asia, and Africa as clover leaves with Jerusalem in the center; the map of the Americas made by a smear of jam on a cutting board; or the map of physics that presents the various branches as rivers and the great physicists as villages. Jacobs's followers seem fascinated with the paradox between the order one generally associates with maps and the wild flights of imagination some cartographers have taken. Millions have viewed *Strange Maps*, which generated a book of the same name.

The passion with which Jacobs writes about these maps makes it clear that he is on his way home with this pursuit. He shows us that paradox can be endlessly fascinating and endlessly motivating. You can use paradox to find home and to keep you on your way there. What juxtapositions fascinate you and move you to action? When you consider one thing and its seeming opposite, does this combination call to you in a special way? If so, you know where you're going.

A wake-up call that sends you home

The Essentials all contribute to Always Be on Your Way Home in distinctive ways. Curiosity lets you see beyond your personal borders. Openness gives you the chance to find what is precisely (as opposed to generally) right for you. Sensuality helps you to feel when you're on your way and when you're not. And paradox creates opportunities to get a vision of home through the lens of seemingly opposite things.

In turn, Always Be on Your Way Home is a process that leads directly to the development and deepening of your self-story. It's nearly impossible to have a vital self-story without a sense of home. How can you know what you are about if you can't identify where you are meant to be? When you're going where you're supposed to be going, your self-story gains in precision immeasurably.

A useful way of illustrating this is to see the effect identifying and heading home had on a public personality. Ray LaMontagne is a Grammy Award–winning singer-songwriter who tours regularly and plays to large crowds. However, even though his father was a musician, LaMontagne had no aspirations of becoming one when he was growing up. Since his parents split when he was young and he moved around a great deal, life might simply have been too onerous to entertain such notions.

"It was difficult and it was at times very scary to grow up in a household so unsettled and at times very violent," he told an interviewer. "But, it also . . . I guess it earned me a sort of wisdom at a young age that's served me well."

When he was finally out on his own, he gravitated toward Maine, his primary goal being survival rather than advancement.

"It's a scrappy, scruffy place," he said of Maine to NPR. "A lot of people struggling to keep things going, to make ends meet, which was why I was there, because you can. If you're a struggling tradesman, you can go to Maine and make ends meet . . . just barely."

He wound up in a shoe factory, working sixty-five-hour weeks to earn a living. At one point while he was doing this, his clock radio awakened him with Stephen Stills's song "Treetop Flyer" and something clicked. Right then, he decided that his future was about being a singer-songwriter, that this was what he was really meant to do. He took the day off work, bought the Stills album on which the song appeared, and listened to it repeatedly. While he'd never played an instrument before, he bought a guitar and taught himself these songs. Eventually he moved on to writing his own.

"I didn't know what I was doing; I just knew I could. It took a long time to allow myself to sing."

LaMontagne realized where he was supposed to be going and he started heading home. He put together a demo and then shopped it to record labels. It took five years, but in 2004, RCA released his first album, *Trouble.* Three other full-length albums have followed, along with many tours, much acclaim, and that Grammy.

Once Ray LaMontagne understood the direction he needed to be going, his self-story coalesced. He was headed toward his true destination and he started living life at an entirely new level.

The same can happen to each of us if we can point ourselves toward home and allow ourselves to be on a perpetual journey to get there.

chapter seven

Own Your Narrative

MICHAEL LEE is the founder of Phoenix Rising Yoga Therapy, an acclaimed international yoga program. He has given the keynote at the World Yoga Symposium, and his work has been published in *Yoga Journal*. Phoenix Rising is distinctive in a number of ways, including the use of practitioner-assisted yoga postures (a teacher helps you into and helps you hold the poses) and a strong emphasis on deep introspection. What distinguishes it most, though, is a process that Lee refers to as "the Edge."

"I was living in an ashram in the early eighties," he told me, "and I committed to doing a daily yoga practice for a year and a quarter. It was the same routine every day, but I realized that if you thought it was the same old practice every day, you weren't looking deep enough. I needed to go into the experience a little more deeply and detect the nuances. One morning, I was just noticing myself struggling around trying to be a little more effortful in the postures and trying to push myself a little harder, and it was really pissing me off. I'd look around and there were so many people who were more adept than I was—there was all this mind chatter going on.

"This happened for about three or four days in a row and I decided, the hell with it, I'm just going to play with it. Rather than try to push the edge, I backed off a little bit and I held it there. I thought, 'This is not quite too much,' and I kept trying to find that fine point where it wasn't too much and it wasn't not enough. And I discovered it! And when I discovered it, it was an amazing experience. All my anger went away, and I began to feel kind of ecstatic."

What Lee had found was the *exact* place where he should be holding his postures so that he could get the most from them that he was capable of getting. Having practiced self-awareness for years, he soon came to understand that what he'd uncovered had greater ramifications.

"It dawned on me when I was doing some journaling: You know, that's sort of a metaphor for my life. That's how I live my life. I'm always trying to get to the next mountain, I'm always trying to push and struggle and make life hard work, and it doesn't really have to be that way. I started to look at that and apply it to different areas of my life with very similar results. It gave me a lot more joy, it gave me a lot more freedom, and I really believe it made me more effective.

"For example, one of the things for me was going out of my way to impress people. I always believed that people had to think I'm okay. They've got to think I'm worthwhile or I'm good. I realized I didn't need to do that and backed off a bit, finding that edge where I'm engaging but not engaging with too much persuasion or force or effort. What I found was people would warm more to me. I was making more friends. I was making friends with people who were in powerful places because I wasn't trying. It wasn't that I was making no effort. There was an edge there, but it wasn't too much and it wasn't too little."

Once Lee understood this, he realized that he could help others experience the same evolution. During our conversation, he recounted how he'd spent years in organizational development consulting trying to help people to look at what wasn't working, respond to feedback, and shift to more effective behavior. What he'd found was that people could have a temporary transformational moment at a workshop or conference, but the effects rarely lasted once that person went back to his or her normal environment. These people might feel as though they'd made some kind of progress, but what really manifests is what Lee calls "the same old new me." By incorporating the Edge into his yoga teaching, he found a breakthrough.

"I believe the body-mind connection is a very powerful part of the change process. When you can feel something viscerally in your body and then connect that experience to how you show up in your life, then that's a very powerful message. It gets my attention more quickly and more easily, and makes it easier for me to accept the awareness and make a decision to move on it.

"Someone can facilitate the physical part of the experience, they can help people find their edge, and they can help them dialogue with themselves once they reach that part. It's about using the Edge in a physical sense and conducting a dialogue around what is occurring in the moment as it is happening, and then trying to figure out how this connects with your life. Sometimes you can and sometimes you can't. If someone is really open to self-inquiry, it's going to work a lot better than if they aren't.

"First we'll have a conversation about what your intentions

are, what you want to do with your life. Depending on your background in yoga we will then structure assisted yoga postures. We'll guide your body through two or three different yoga postures and teach you how to find your edge and teach you how to be present, to focus your awareness at those places. There will be a sequence of sessions until you start to feel more comfortable about really engaging your awareness and detecting the nuances between thoughts, feelings, and body sensations."

What Lee also understands is that the Edge is not a particular place, but a destination of constant evolution. The exact spot between too much and not enough changes as a person changes.

"The Edge can be moving on a daily basis, depending on how you meet yourself on that particular day."

Michael Lee has found a way to connect a philosophy across physical, spiritual, and emotional domains. He and the other thousand or so Phoenix Rising practitioners are helping people to discover the place where they are most right, where they are most completely and actively themselves. Through a physical process, he's helping people to connect with their self-stories and use those self-stories to be the actualized version of themselves.

"I believe that we all look for connection to something beyond what we are aware of, even if we don't know it," Lee says on the Phoenix Rising website. "Generally, we try to find it outside of ourselves. Luckily I was able to find it from the inside and bring it to the world as well, although at times during the journey I have had regrets about ever starting it. The inner path is not an easy one, and I have experienced more growth from my work with Phoenix Rising Yoga Therapy than I would have ever wanted in several lifetimes. But if I ask myself has it been worth it the answer is always a resounding 'Yes.'"

Michael Lee is getting at something very powerful and illuminating. It's a variation on a process that I've come to know as Own Your Narrative.

Owning you

As you already know, self-story is not a chronicle of the events in your life or even the background to those events or the context in which they took place. Self-story is *what you are about*. Having a clear sense of what you are about offers a variety of benefits, but maybe even more important is that once you uncover your self-story, you make it an intrinsic part of you, that you live with and for that story—you own it. That, in turn (and we'll get to this in a few pages), makes your self-story stronger.

Michael Lee's notion of the Edge fascinates me, because in many ways it is a metaphor for owning your narrative. Lee teaches people to find yoga postures that are neither too strenuous nor too easy; they are precisely right for that person. In a sense, therefore, those postures come to represent the person doing them, since no one else would employ that exact level of effort. Owning your narrative requires a similar process. It's about testing and monitoring your self-story until you discover one that feels like an ideal fit—and then wearing that self-story like a second set of clothing.

Let's go back for a minute to Debra Byrd, whom we met in chapter five. During our talk, Byrd revealed much of her self-story to me. She's an optimist with a rock-and-roll heart. Obviously, I'm oversimplifying here, and none of us have self-stories that streamlined. However, it was clear to me not only that Byrd was aware of her narrative and owning it but also that she'd come to this narrative after some careful examination. She'd tested her optimism against some considerable challenges, including working for a criminal. She'd also come to realize that she was a rock and roller even though she'd been trained in and had a tremendous amount of respect for opera. For Byrd, owning her narrative means living with and enacting who she is. This has led her to follow a career in pop music and also to serving as something of a dream maker for contestants on musical competitions, helping them to refine their skills and believe in their possibilities.

Obviously, before you can own your narrative, you need to understand what your narrative is. As we discussed that at length earlier, I'm not going to go into it again here. However, I think it is important to briefly address what your narrative is not: It is not conditional. I was speaking recently with someone who casually mentioned that he's "a different person" when he's with the other members of his family. This man is the youngest among a large group of siblings, and while he presents himself as an innovative entrepreneur in business situations and a raconteur and natural leader in social ones, he becomes quiet and submissive around his brothers and sisters because, even though he's in his forties, they still make him feel like a kid.

This person has failed as yet to own his narrative. If you truly own your narrative, you never become someone else. Of course, different parts of your personality might emerge at different times, and certainly all of us need to adjust for social situations (even if not all of us do so as often as we should), but if you truly own your narrative, you are *yourself* in all circumstances. You're not the life of the party in one setting and a wallflower in another. You're never a thought leader who can't utter a single intelligent sentence when certain people are in the room. Unless your self-story is at the level beyond roles and specific situations, it's too labile. If you're really at the point where you have a self-story that's authentic and motivating, then it shouldn't ever be shaken by roles.

Owning your narrative means that you have a clear enough picture of what you are about that you are always you no matter where you are or what you're doing. There's a small collection of very popular food markets in the Connecticut/New York area named Stew Leonard's. As you walk into a Stew Leonard's store, you come up against a bold statement about the store's customer service policy:

Rule 1:
The customer is always right!

Rule 2:
If the customer is ever wrong, reread Rule 1!

When thinking about owning your narrative, you might seek a variation on this axiom:

Rule 1:
You are always you!

Rule 2:
If you ever feel that you aren't you, reread Rule 1!

Of course, I would add to Rule 2 that if you ever feel that you aren't you, you might first need to make sure that you are who you think you are.

This is not to say that owning your narrative means that you've come to a point where you're no longer evolving. Just as Always Be on Your Way Home isn't meant to suggest that your objective is to *get* home, Own Your Narrative isn't meant to suggest that your narrative is a fixed thing. Part of owning your narrative is understanding that it is an ongoing one. Your self-story is a continuing story that might take you in surprising directions, though it should never take you in contradictory directions. As such, owning your narrative means that you accept that the narrative is going to evolve as you do.

Owning up and shouting out

One of the most effective ways to achieve ownership of your narrative is to see how it holds up to a challenge. A most telling challenge is to juxtapose your narrative with the version of the narrative that others have for you. With this in mind, I've always wanted to run an extensive study of reunions, because they allow for an environment in which people see reflected in others a version of who they once were. For example, when you go to your twentieth high school reunion, you will likely see several people who know nothing more about you now than they did twenty years ago (this is still true even with the proliferation of social media). When they meet up with you now, they're likely to reflect back to you their memories of you from two decades earlier, and in doing so they give you a version of yourself that butts up against your personal narrative.

I have yet to perform this study in a scientific way, because I've never had the free time or the available funding to do the extensive work necessary. However, I did recently ask a professional writers organization to share some of their reunion memories, and their responses were both entertaining and illuminating.

"I was at a high school reunion—my tenth, and the first one I'd attended," says novelist Lisa Verge Higgins. "I'd finished college, got a degree in chemistry, tried out graduate school, worked as a chemist for five years, and, to the bewilderment of my college and work friends who'd known me only as a scientist, published my first and second novels. At the time of the reunion, I was at a crossroads, trying to decide whether I wanted to go back to graduate school or take a crack at writing for a living. I spoke to a good friend I'd fallen out of touch with and I confessed my dilemma. She did not seem surprised by the fact that I'd published novels—she reminded me of a creative writing class we'd taken together, how we used to read voraciously, her memory of my childhood bedroom full of books. She said to me, 'I always knew you were going to be a writer.'"

Novelist Jennifer Stevenson has a fascinating memory about meeting up with people she'd known when she was on the roller derby circuit:

"I was in roller derby from age fifty-two to age fifty-four—a very, very late bloomer—and kicked out for being too old. Derby changed my life, made an athlete of me, made me proud of my big ass and my giant legs for what they could do—hip-check you into next week—not for how they looked in a short skirt. I still looked like a hausfrau but, oh baby, what I could do with it. That was several years ago. Occasionally, I run into skaters I knew back then at a local bout or at a tournament. They're always pretty surprised that I'm still skating. They're almost all thirty years younger than I am or more, and many of them have retired due to injuries or just getting a life. I speed-skate now—won a national bronze medal two years ago, in fact. At first I wasn't revising my sense of self at these reunions. I simply felt that the kids were underestimating old broads. Now I'm questioning a lot of things. Is it weird that about twelve hundred women over age forty across the country skate roller derby? What does it say about our culture that most women my age are on multiple medications and would never willingly work out? Will I ever find a doctor who doesn't try to talk me into slowing down?"

Novelist Sharon Ihle told me, "I attended my fiftieth high school reunion last year and discovered something about my classmates, the 'in crowd.' I was fairly anonymous during my high school years, not part of the in crowd, but happy enough with my own circle of friends. I hadn't seen most of those people in over twenty-five years when I arrived at this reunion. That oh-so-fabulous in crowd didn't pay much attention to me in school or twenty-five years ago (as in before I was a published author), but at the fiftieth, I found I was suddenly someone to be fawned over. It made me laugh, inwardly at that—but laugh I did."

Novelist Trish Jensen has a funny little memory that is very poignant in its own way:

"At my last reunion my old boyfriend (captain of the football team), who later dumped me and married the beauty queen (because, as he told me then, 'You're cute, but she's beautiful'), came up to me and we talked about prom night, etc. He kept staring at

me and I finally said, '*What?* What are you staring at?' His answer was, 'Apparently cute has a longer shelf life.'"

Each of these stories involves a different opportunity for owning one's narrative. In Lisa Verge Higgins's case, the reunion experience came at a life-defining inflection point, a moment when she
was literally trying to figure out who she was. Her narrative was at
a crossroads, and she didn't feel she could follow both paths. By
meeting up with someone who had always seen her as a writer, she
was able to understand that this had been an essential part of her
self-story all along, making the decision much easier for her.

Jennifer Stevenson's reunion experiences offered her affirma-
tion of another sort—that the distinctive narrative she's created
for herself is worth owning and worth shouting about. What
comes across in Stevenson's tale is that she prides herself on being
a one-in-a-million person (her derby name is Flash Hottie, which
says quite a bit). When she meets people from her roller derby
past, their memories of her and the context into which they put
her underscore just how effective she's been at accomplishing this.

What happened at Sharon Ihle's fiftieth reunion allowed her
to look at her narrative through the prism of the narratives of
others. "At that reunion I didn't make a major discovery about
how much I'd evolved," she told me. "I marveled at how little the
in crowd had evolved." This is, of course, an extremely important
observation. Sometimes the most effective way to bolster your
narrative—and therefore allow yourself to take full ownership of
it—is to let others bolster it for you. What Ihle saw in the relative
lack of evolution from her former schoolmates was an unspoken
confirmation that her own evolution had been considerable.

Trish Jensen's story is good for a laugh, but how she interpreted
the experience speaks volumes. "I thought that was hilarious," she

told me, "but it can be extrapolated to anything. 'Smart has a longer shelf life.' 'Determination has a longer shelf life.'" Meeting this old boyfriend allowed Jensen to test her narrative against his impression of her. "Cute" wasn't an important part of her narrative, but her ability to extrapolate from this to things that are foundations of her narrative meant that she has a strong sense of her self-story and that she feels very good about owning it.

The quest for you

Your Essentials work in concert to generate the process of Own Your Narrative, and in so doing they enhance your self-story.

Curiosity works at a fundamental level in helping you to own your narrative, as it allows you to explore and examine a variety of personas until you find the one that you truly connect with. For you to truly take ownership of your narrative, though, curiosity is required to perform another function: discovering your most fundamental core values. A narrative you can own is one that can't be shaken from you. What are those values for you?

One of the most extreme ways of identifying your fundamental values through intensive use of curiosity is the vision quest. This is definitely not for most people, but it does highlight the process in dramatic ways. The traditional vision quest is a ritual used by many Native American cultures to help individuals find their true purpose. It typically involves a long journey alone into the wilderness with very few supplies, fasting for days, and long stretches of meditation and reaching out to nature spirits. The object of the quest is for participants to strip down to their most basic selves in order to discover their roles in life.

Several organizations offer assistance in performing a vision quest. One such organization is Rites of Passage, in Santa Rosa, California. Their process involves participants starting the quest with a small group of others and then heading into the wilderness alone, fasting for three or four days. "As your thoughts begin to empty out," they say on their website, "you can look into the pool of your own being, noticing how you are, what your dreams are made of, what you need to let go of."

"It has been ten days since our return from the Vision Quest," participant Christina Thorn wrote to Rites of Passage, "and I am pleasantly surprised with the differences I continue to find at work and at home. I am aware that the circumstances of my life have not changed, but my perspective is radically different. There have always been opportunities for improvement in my life, areas that weren't quite working to their full potential. Something about the program gave me not only the gift of awareness, but the tools on how to let go of what was previously holding me back. Many limiting beliefs I held on my life, my marriage, and my career were left in the desert at the end of our journey."

"Doing a Vision Quest is an enormous help in overcoming one or more mental or emotional blockages or diseases," said Dr. Tony Burlingham, another participant. "By accessing the infinite healing energy of the earth, by living with it unencumbered by food and other normal burdens of everyday life, and combining it with one's own resources, you gain virtually infinite healing energy to change one's state of mind. I find to a large extent this is a permanent change for the better, not just a temporary buzz."

Obviously, such an undertaking is inconceivable for most of us, and I'm certainly not suggesting that you try it. However, at its core the vision quest shows us a way to use our curiosity in the service of owning our narratives. The object of the vision quest is to dig deep, to explore yourself at a level that might not be possible while you're inundated with your everyday intrusions. Can you do this without skipping food for four days, while still sleeping on a comfortable mattress at night, and without the sound of wolves baying in the distance? I believe so, if you're curious enough. I believe it comes down to employing the goal of the vision quest, if not all the methods. Certainly, introspection is critical, and I believe it starts with this question: What am I willing to give up and what must I absolutely hold on to at all costs? If you can put yourself in the position to answer that question with complete honesty—even if you're doing it with a glass of wine in your hand and Coltrane playing in the background, though most people require something more strenuous to force the issue—you'll have gone a long way toward owning your narrative.

Running toward you

Owning your narrative requires being in intimate contact with it. This is where sensuality comes in. As we've discussed, two of the critical components of this process are understanding that your true narrative is inviolate and understanding that it is always evolving. Sensuality can help you with both of these. By being in touch with all of your senses, you come to distinguish between feeling that something is a temporary setback and feeling that your life has gone dramatically off track.

Psychotherapist Bob Livingstone offers a surprisingly physical approach to dealing with self-examination in his book *The Body Mind Soul Solution*. In it, Livingstone advocates asking yourself vital questions while exercising to take advantage of the mind-clearing benefits that physical labor provides.

"Exercise in itself elevates you to a calm reflective state," Livingstone writes in the book's introduction. "Exercise combined with self-questioning as regards emotional pain can bond to the healing power of the higher self. The wedding of the mind and body to the higher place will provide reassuring answers to these painful questions. You will discover, too, that you can retain and enjoy this connection to your higher self for a longer period of time while you are exercising than when you're at rest. The changes in brain chemistry that occur while exercising can explain scientifically why this state of reflective and receptive calmness is induced. But there is also the magic of the experience that transpires when you combine exercise and self-questioning. You may have been emotionally 'stuck' for many years, and suddenly, in a revelatory flash, you feel hopeful that your life can change. As you begin to understand why you have been stuck, you will develop ways to move on. You will be renewed."

Livingstone provides a dramatic example of the process from his own life:

I awoke from one of those truncated sleeps and stumbled across the bedroom to where my running clothes hung. I slowly put them on in the early morning darkness. I was sleep deprived, my body ached from sleeping at a bad angle, and my head was beating with a sinus flare-up. I really needed to work out.

I put Mary J. Blige's *Dance for Me* album on my MP3 player. I really wanted to absorb its energy. As I began my five-mile run, with the music flowing into my ears, I started thinking about everything that was bothering me. I silently asked myself, "What is upsetting me right now?" But I did not press myself for an answer. I simply found my running rhythm and allowed patience to rule the hour.

Then suddenly they came, in the form of a memory.

A recollection of a happier time several years before flashed upon my mind. My wife and I had been taking care of a little girl, Laura, on weekends and on vacations. She had always seemed connected to me spiritually, and I recalled the fun we had together laughing and listening to music. I enjoyed reading to her at night and teaching her how to read, cook, play sports and behave in good restaurants. At that moment of recollection I realized how much I really loved that little girl. We'd been helping her aunt raise her, but one day her aunt had a falling-out with us over a disagreement on her child-rearing methods and we were never allowed to take care of her again. The door was shut in our face and there was nothing we could do about it. The pain of this remembered loss took away my breath as I continued running. The tears that streamed down my face mixed with the sweat that flowed from my pores.

Once the run was over, I was pleased that I was able to connect with my feelings surrounding the loss of Laura. I was also surprised that this loss affected me so deeply, for

I thought I had worked through this problem. I had no idea it still troubled me. Then I wondered if possibly, the combination of exercise and self-examination over what was troubling me had allowed the blocked feelings to surface.

What Bob Livingstone is getting at are the breakthroughs that are possible to achieve when you employ your senses to address what you're feeling deep inside. While his methods are directed at helping a person address emotional pain, it's easy to extrapolate here. This is a strong testament to the value of using your senses to connect with your narrative and then own it.

Capturing my contradictions

The contribution that paradox makes to Own Your Narrative is in helping you to refine it to something that is precisely yours, much in the way that Michael Lee's Edge enhances self-definition. When you identify and contemplate the paradoxes in your life and where you fall on the line between the extremes created by those paradoxes, you identify yourself at a delightfully precise level. Let me tell a personal story here to explain what I mean.

Many years ago, the first woman I went out with after my divorce from my first wife was someone I met while doing some consulting for the Bureau of Indian Affairs when I was living in Washington, D.C. I found myself attracted to her instantly, not only because of her beauty, but also because she had a certain gravitas about her. I could just tell that she saw things that most people missed. We talked for a few minutes after a meeting, and I invited her to join me for lunch the next day.

At lunch, we were sitting side by side in a banquette. At that point, we'd only known each other from the meeting, the brief conversation afterward, and the chatting we'd done while waiting for our food. I noticed that she was looking at me quizzically, so I asked her about it.

"You're a strange person," she said. "You are the most opinionated person . . . and the most open."

I'd never had someone recognize this so clearly. "You're right," I said. "And it's not a contradiction for me."

While she was the first person to say this to me, it was something about myself I was already aware of, and I consider this paradox to be a fundamental part of my narrative. I am most definitely opinionated, and as you probably have noticed in this book by now, I have no problems sharing my opinions with everyone. However, I am also extremely open and utterly fascinated by the idea that I might learn something today that I didn't know yesterday. For me, these two extremes work in the service of each other. I'm opinionated because I spend my life observing the world from an anthropological perspective, which requires me to be open, and I'm open because I need as much input as possible to learn more about myself by understanding how I feel about the opinions of others.

This paradox is one of many I embrace in the ownership of my narrative. Exploring your own paradoxes—the ways in which you manifest one thing and its seeming opposite, and where you sit comfortably between those two things—is a key step in owning yours.

A tap on the shoulder

Speaking of openness, this Essential offers a considerable boost to Own Your Narrative by allowing you to see the nuances in your self-story that could very possibly become central components of your narrative. Openness allows you to invite into your life possibilities that might be uniquely fulfilling and right for you, but that you might miss if you aren't willing to let such possibilities in.

Bryant Austin had been a wildlife photographer for more than forty years when he went diving in Tonga. During this expedition, he spotted a humpback whale calf and moved closer and closer to it until he was no more than six feet away. As he studied the majestic creature, he felt a tap on his shoulder. He turned to find himself in *very* close contact with the humpback's mother. The mother didn't seem to be overly concerned that Austin was there; she just wanted him to know that she was watching.

That moment of connection changed Austin from a wildlife photographer to a wildlife photographer with a cause. Realizing that virtually no one on the planet had ever had the chance to experience whales on their scale—his biography states, "Less than one millionth of one percent of the human population will experience what Austin has witnessed"—he decided to create life-size photographs. His largest is six feet by thirty feet, and all of them present a sense of proportion that can't help but change one's perception about these creatures.

"I'm trying to give people a memory, a sense of what they're like, to really see them in this way, not only on their scale but these calm, mindful gazes, these expressions in their eyes," Austin told an interviewer.

Austin realized that his work had the power to change opinions, and it became his mission to do so. He started the nonprofit Marine Mammal Conservation Through the Arts to address an area of great concern for him. The whaling industry has had a profound effect on whale populations, and some species are nearing extinction. Through his huge-format presentations, Austin is making whales more real to those who might not have previously understood how powerful their presence is. The photos are dramatic, but Austin is touching hearts and changing minds in more ways than one.

"I'm finding that the photographs are actually secondary. It's the relationships that I have with individual whales. The amount of time I spend with these whales to gain their interest or trust to produce these photographs is what audiences are finding most compelling about them."

It's unlikely that Bryant Austin had a refinement of his narrative in mind when he went into the water that day in Tonga. By his own admission, he "never wanted to be a storyteller; I never wanted to be a public speaker." However, by being open, he found his narrative growing in dramatic ways, and he has taken full ownership of that.

This is a vital step in owning your narrative. By being open, you can find the next level of your narrative. You can go from the generic to the specific, until you find a story that is uniquely yours—and that you can own proudly.

As is true of each of the five processes we're discussing in the second portion of this book, the process leads to a considerable enhancement of your self-story. This may never be truer than it is with Own Your Narrative. The ways in which the Essentials contribute to this particular process facilitate—and, in fact, demand—refinement of your self-story. As you begin to own your narrative, you will discover what is most important to you through curiosity, stay on the right course through sensuality, discover your precise place through paradox, and find the particular nuances that truly define you through openness. Each of these sharpens you and deepens you. Taking ownership of who you are not only ratifies your narrative, but it runs it through a battery of tests that makes it stronger.

That's the message that becomes clear when you look at how the process affected Michael Lee or Bryant Austin, or even me. By owning our narratives, we emerged more fully into the world. This is a critical step in accomplishment, fulfillment, and happiness.

chapter eight

Stop and Focus

EVEN TODAY, AND even in the most populous state in America, it's possible for you not to carry the entire world in your pocket. Troy Wolverton, personal technology columnist for the *San Jose Mercury News*, learned that on a recent family trip—much to his delight.

For their vacation in the summer of 2012, he and his family decided to go camping for six days at Lassen Volcanic National Park, in California. Lassen was appealing to them because it has four volcanoes and all sorts of hydrothermal activity. What it doesn't have, however, is something that Wolverton had become very accustomed to being with all the time—cell service.

"Because I'm a technology reviewer," he told me, "I have loaner devices for smartphones, and I had a number of devices with me. Before we left, I went online to check what our coverage would be because I figured we'd want to have some kind of connection to the outside world. It looked like AT&T would have service. When we got out there, the first sign that we weren't going to have service was that we stopped getting coordinates to our GPS. By the time we got to our actual campsite, we had absolutely no service. I thought maybe if we hiked to the top of one of the volcanoes we could see if there was any. There was none."

At this point, many people today might have panicked at the idea that they were cut off from communication, from social media, from their stock prices. Wolverton didn't panic; however, he did see it as an inconvenience.

"It wasn't like I was going to be surfing the web while I was there, but I did want to at least let my parents know that we had made it safely and to be able to send pictures."

A drive to another part of the park allowed him to tell his parents that everything was okay and that they shouldn't expect to hear from him. After that, he and his family settled into spending a little time off the grid.

"It didn't take very long to adjust. While I was hoping to have service there, the whole idea of the vacation was not to sit down in front of our devices. The point was to get away from things, go hiking, and explore the woods. And there wasn't anything we could do about it. We were far enough away that I couldn't simply walk a hundred yards and get service. We just had to deal with the fact that we didn't have a connection.

"It was liberating. I feel like if you've got a computer or a smartphone, it's always there. It's become a reflex to grab it when you have a spare second or when there's a question at the table that stumps you. It's become a daily part of your life. In some ways that's very cool. But it seems like my attention and my wife's attention is frequently diverted to these devices, and I often feel that I'm not devoting enough attention to my wife or my kids because the device is right there and it's hard to put it down.

"When we were in Lassen, there was less of a compulsion to pick it up because you couldn't do anything with it anyway. From that standpoint, it was relaxing to be able to focus on the kids. The problem with the device is that you pick it up and you've gotten fifty different e-mail messages. One of the stresses of modern life is all of the e-mail that piles up. You feel like you have to clean it out before it stacks up too high. One of the evil things about these devices is that you wind up working a lot more than you would otherwise."

Since using devices wasn't an available option, Wolverton allowed himself to turn his attention to the pleasure of his family's company and the wonders of the world around him.

"With no signal and thus no way to check e-mail or access IMDb, we spent more time conversing, enjoying the scenery, watching the stars at night, and grappling with the tasks of camping, such as starting the campfire and getting dinner going," he wrote in an article about the experience for the *Mercury News*. "I was more relaxed and spent more quality time with my wife and kids. Heck, I was even able to smell the flowers, in this case a wonderfully fragrant field of lupine. I can't wait to do it again."

One of the things Wolverton noticed was that once he was back in cell range, his blood pressure began to rise as he started going through his e-mail. This was in stark contrast to the experience he'd just been through, during which he felt more relaxed than he'd been in a long time. Without the ability to stay in touch with work and outside distractions, he'd been able to let all of it go—and he not only survived the experience, but he thrived.

Since returning from Lassen, Wolverton has tried to make some time on the weekend when he abandons his phone. He isn't always successful, but he's cognizant of the value of doing so.

"I think it is good to get away. It was certainly good for me to unplug and to be disconnected. I think the main thing is being aware of how addictive and attached to these devices we can be and trying to find ways to carve out time away from them. I think it was good for me to be away from it for days."

Being off the grid temporarily allowed Troy Wolverton to stop his normal behaviors and focus exclusively on his wife and children. It was an edifying experience that he plans to repeat regularly, and one that serves as a valuable model for one of our five processes.

> He who can no longer pause to wonder and stand
> rapt in awe, is as good as dead; his eyes are closed.
>
> —Albert Einstein

Taking the escalator to the next level

We spend a tremendous amount of our time reacting to our lives. In fact, it has become increasingly possible in our society to do nothing but react. Certainly, there's enough to react *to*. There's the endless stimulus beamed to us through the devices Troy Wolverton was talking about. There are our work responsibilities, our family responsibilities, our social responsibilities. There are dinners to cook, PTO meetings to attend, phone calls to return, television shows to watch, and games of *Temple Quest* to play. With everything coming at us, it's easy to feel like a hockey goalie blocking an endless number of shots in an effort to keep the other team from winning.

The problem with this, though, is that, like that goalie, if we're only reacting, we aren't doing anything to advance the score of the game ourselves. Doing that requires a different action.

Actually, it requires inaction.

The only way to go beyond where you are right now, and therefore the only way to grow as a person and live a more fulfilled life, is to employ the process of Stop and Focus. Being in the mode of perpetual reaction might prevent you from falling behind, but it will never move you forward. To move forward, you need to have at least a momentary stop, a time when you can scan where you are and take account.

Being able to step out of the normal flow of your life to focus allows you to see certain details that are not necessarily apparent otherwise. It gives you just enough perspective on what you're doing to let you see patterns and trends that can lead to breakthroughs. Otherwise, it would be extremely easy for potentially transformative moments to pass you by without transforming you in any way.

I had a near miss with this recently that was instructive to me. I was working in Manhattan on a consulting project and had a rare free night. I decided to take myself to the movies to see *Beasts of the Southern Wild*, a film I'd been hearing many positive things about. The film, which chronicles the experiences of

Hushpuppy, a six-year-old girl in New Orleans who loses her mother and lives through the ravages of Hurricane Katrina, was every bit as artful and moving as I'd heard. It was transporting, as all good moviemaking is. However, I did not expect it to be as illuminating as it turned out to be.

This illumination nearly passed me by. I'd seen the movie at the Lincoln Plaza Cinemas, which requires taking an escalator down below street level to get to the theater. As I was heading up and out afterward, I'd already started thinking about the work project I was in the middle of and the meetings I had scheduled for the next day. Images from the movie were playing in the background for me, though, and I decided it might be worthwhile to stop and focus on them. When I did so, I realized that what the little girl had gone through resonated so strongly with me because, like her, I'd dealt with a profound loss—the death of my father—at a similar age. By the time I got off the escalator, I knew that I needed to take this deeper, to understand why this story had moved me in such a deeply personal way. It struck me that Hushpuppy had confronted the trauma in her life much more directly than I had and that, all these years later, I still needed to finish dealing with this. As I headed back onto the street, I realized that I would need to take steps to address my unresolved business very soon, and I started processing that immediately.

The experience changed me and led to some closure that had been very long in coming. Yet I might have missed it if I'd decided to check the messages on my iPhone when I left the theater instead of stopping and focusing.

Not every instance of stopping and focusing is going to be

this profound. Sometimes you'll stop what you're doing, think about it for a few minutes, and decide that painting the bathroom blue is a better choice than painting it yellow. However, there is always something to be gained from allowing yourself the opportunity to take a step back from what you're doing to *consider* what you're doing.

> Sometimes you need to press pause to let everything sink in.
>
> —Sebastian Vettel, Formula 1 race car driver

Mindless

The ability to focus is a tremendous contributor to performance. Distractions, after all, distract, and if you are capable of diminishing those distractions, you're likely to do whatever you're doing better.

Distractions come in numerous forms—colleagues, electronic devices, your dog, your growling stomach—but perhaps the distractions most detrimental to performance are one's own thoughts. This is amply illustrated in the field of sports. I've spoken to many sports psychologists over the years, and I've heard repeatedly that among professional athletes, the range of athletic ability is fairly narrow. What distinguishes the Super Bowl champion quarterback from the one who throws three interceptions in his team's most important game of the season is often a matter of focus. I'm reminded of the Kevin Costner movie *For Love of the Game*, in which Costner's character, Billy Chapel, is a hugely successful but aging baseball pitcher. Before each pitch, Chapel tells himself to "close the mechanism," which is his tool for driving thoughts of the crowd, his teammates, and even the batter out of his mind so he can execute the pitch he needs to execute.

A recent *Psychology Today* article addressed a study in which cyclists were asked to go as quickly as possible over a virtual two-thousand-meter course. Each participant cycled the course five times, but the final time, they were told that they'd be racing against an opponent, who would be visible to them as an avatar on the screen. The avatar actually represented the fastest previous time the cyclist had run, and in twelve of fourteen cases, the cyclists beat the avatars, even though, by this point, they were physically exhausted from having done four other trials. Lead researcher Jo Corbett stated that the results stemmed from the racers' ability to focus on the competition rather than how tired they were, tapping into an anaerobic energy reserve.

British sports psychologist Simon Hartley equates focus with a narrow "torch" (flashlight) beam, saying it's the athlete's job to "decide where the beam will shine." He recalls working with a British Olympic team shortly after they competed unsuccessfully in Beijing in 2008. The first thing he did was ask the team's coach to name the five most significant factors that would affect the team's performance. The coach couldn't stop naming things until he'd come up with thirty-two—at which point Hartley realized that the coach had been loading down the minds of his athletes until they couldn't possibly focus effectively.

"A tennis player should arguably be one hundred percent focused on the ball," he said in an article for *Podium Sports*

Journal. "If she's not watching the ball, the chances of playing a decent shot are pretty remote. If the player is thinking about making a mistake with the last shot (instead of shining their torch on the ball) her torch will be shining on her own thoughts. When we overthink, we experience what I call 'thought blindness.' Imagine a batsman in cricket facing a fast bowler who delivers a ball at ninety mph. The batsman has to select a shot and execute it in a split second. Thinking takes a relatively long time. If the batsman thinks, he will not see the ball clearly because his brain will be tied up with his thoughts and will not be registering the ball. The only way for the batsman to play a good shot is to simply watch the ball as closely as possible and let his unconscious mind play the shot. The batsman has to be in a 'mindless' state."

Earlier in this book, we talked about Jerry West and the long run of basketball success he had with the Los Angeles Lakers. One of those stretches coincided with the time when Phil Jackson was the team's coach. As a coach, Jackson was often referred to as a Zen master or a Jedi. Much of this was because of the emphasis he put on the mental part of the game, including using meditation as a focusing tool. For years, he had a meditation coach for the team, and would often take his players through meditation exercises in which they concentrated on nothing but their breathing for five to ten minutes.

Each of these instances describes a variation on the process of Stop and Focus. In the case of the cyclists, they stopped listening to the messages from their bodies telling them they were too tired to go on and focused instead on their "opponent." What Simon Hartley is advocating is that athletes stop thinking about all but one particular thing, focusing all of their effort on doing that thing masterfully. With the Lakers, meditation provided a tool for getting out of their heads and simply doing, taking a breath, and getting centered. In every case, the process was about ridding themselves of distractions and focusing exclusively on the task at hand.

> Thinking is the place where intelligent actions begin. We pause long enough to look more carefully at a situation, to see more of its character, to think about why it's happening, to notice how it's affecting us and others.
>
> —Margaret J. Wheatley, management consultant

Calling you to a halt

As with the other processes, each of the Essentials contributes to Stop and Focus. Curiosity compels you forward, driving you to take the requisite pause that allows you to concentrate on a particular thing. When I had my revelatory moment after seeing *Beasts of the Southern Wild*, it was curiosity that drove me to follow the initial notion that what I'd seen in the film might have unusual relevance to my own life.

An elegant representation of the connection between curiosity and Stop and Focus is the punctuation mark known as the colon. When a colon appears in a sentence, it is there to pique curiosity. It is an announcement to readers that something especially significant lies on the other side. The colon is in many ways the symbol for Stop and Focus. It announces to readers, "Yes, you've gotten into a nice little rhythm over the past few pages, but as the writer I really need to call your attention to what I'm about to say next." Unlike a period, which inspires the briefest of stops before one moves on to the next thought, the colon calls the reader to a halt. As such, it kicks your curiosity into gear and causes you to focus on whatever appears next. (You'll note that I use very few colons in my writing. This is not to suggest that there isn't much to stop and focus on in this book, only that I consider them to be precious commodities not to be parceled out indiscriminately.)

You can think of Stop and Focus as the colon in your personal narrative. It's a way of activating your curiosity during a potentially meaningful juncture. If something is playing in the back of your mind, as the movie did for me, put a colon there, and then pay extra attention to the words that come immediately thereafter. It might be some of your narrative's juiciest material.

The answer is underneath

Openness assists Stop and Focus by providing the device that allows focusing to have potential value. While you often have a clear agenda when you stop and focus, as the athletes did in the exercise we discussed a few pages ago, at other times you only have an inkling. You have a general idea that you want to do something, but the mechanics of doing so escape you. That's where openness comes in. By being open, you allow your focus the opportunity to land in a useful spot.

Before we started working together, my coauthor, Lou Aronica, wrote a book with mind-body practitioner Dr. Rick Levy,
called *Miraculous Health*. In the process of writing the book,
Lou learned many of the meditation and self-hypnosis techniques that Dr. Levy employs in his work. One such technique is
what Levy calls Hypnotic Regression. During Hypnotic Regression, a person, guided by Levy's recorded assistance, enters a
hypnotic state with a specific problem in mind, and then calls on
his subconscious to reveal something from his past that might
shed light on an emotional wound that is causing the problem.

Lou found the technique interesting but didn't have much
call for using it for its intended purpose. However, he was struggling one day to come up with the plot for a short story he'd been
commissioned to write. He had some vague ideas, but nothing
that was coming together as a useful narrative. Reaching for any
tool that might be available to him, he decided to retrofit Dr.
Levy's Hypnotic Regression technique for his purposes, asking
himself how to address the difficulties he was having with the
story's plot before he began the process of self-hypnosis. When
he counted himself out of hypnosis a half hour later, Lou had the
entire structure for the story in place.

What Lou realized was that his revised Hypnotic Regression
approach was effective for him because it used openness in the
service of Stop and Focus. The question he asked himself before
he began gave him an agenda, hypnosis allowed him to do away
with all distractions, and the connection with his subconscious
allowed him to be open to the possible answers to his question.

"This technique really is the mind-body equivalent of Stop
and Focus," Lou told me. "It allows me to take a half hour away

from everything else where I can just give my mind the space to work on one specific goal. I use it all the time now whenever I find myself stuck as a writer, which, sadly, is more often than I would like."

The art of doing nothing

Each of the processes in this book involves understanding that the vitality of the process comes in taking it only as far as it is intended to go. Remember, for example, that Always Be on Your Way Home isn't about actually *arriving* home. With Stop and Focus, the goal of the process is to achieve a level of focus that you can't achieve if you don't take at least a temporary pause. It isn't Stop, Focus, and Act Immediately. Sometimes, as was the case with my revelation on the escalator ride up from *Beasts of the Southern Wild*, the result of the focus will be to realize that you need to act on something in the near future. Sometimes, as happened with Lou, the result of the focus is to discover a path to action that you can put to use. This isn't to suggest that Stop and Focus never results in immediate action. When Kobe Bryant uses a Phil Jackson meditation technique to center himself before shooting a free throw, this is followed *immediately* by the free throw, as the crowd—not to mention his teammates—would probably be upset if he took a few minutes to first consider the implications of what he'd been focusing on. However, I would suggest that in most cases the process is far less likely to involve quick action.

Here's where paradox comes in. The paradox is that you're

doing something to make yourself *not* do something. You're making the sometimes supreme effort to halt your motion for the sake of stepping back enough to understand what you're doing and where you're going. In this way, Stop and Focus is reminiscent of the Tao concept of wu wei, or action through inaction.

Tao Te Ching speaks of wu wei this way:

Less and less is done
Until non-action is achieved.
When nothing is done, nothing is left undone.

Wu wei involves achieving a mind-set that allows you to be in tune with the flow of the world. You're not fighting against the tide but rather syncing up with the natural order so that you can respond to life's challenges organically. Wu wei is meant to be a lifestyle, and in that regard it is considerably more holistic than what I'm suggesting with Stop and Focus. However, there's much to be learned from this paradox.

What wu wei advocates most strongly is the virtue of not trying to make something of the world that can't be made. Taoists will often point to the parable of the pine tree and the willow tree to illustrate this point. The parable looks at these two trees covered in a heavy layer of snow. The pine tree is rigid, and the weight of the snow ultimately causes its branches or even the entire tree to come crashing down. The willow, on the other hand, is flexible. When covered with snow, it bends toward the ground because that's where the snow is taking it, but it does not crack under the strain and therefore returns to form when the snow is gone.

This relates to Stop and Focus in that the desire to always be on, to constantly stay on top of all the input one receives, requires an exhausting level of action that is likely to break quite a few of our branches and maybe even bring us down. When we stop—when we commit to a temporary bout of inaction—we allow the world to do what it will while we gather ourselves.

In this way, paradox serves a vital function in Stop and Focus.

Back from center

Sensuality contributes to the process of Stop and Focus in two ways. One is by giving you the sensual clues that stepping away from your situation might be beneficial. While we certainly need to teach ourselves to stop and focus, to make this part of our ongoing effort toward growth, we also need to teach ourselves to pick up the clues within our bodies that we need to back off a bit. Are you aware of how your body feels when you're getting overwhelmed? Do you feel a catch in your throat, a pain in your lower back, a tingling in your fingers? What are the messages you get from your senses when you need a breather in order to gather yourself? Do you get different physical signals when something significant is happening to you but is threatening to pass you by if you don't give it some serious thought?

The other way that sensuality plays a role in this process is during the focusing phase itself. By being aware of the experience of our own experience, we can gain perspective on our actions and understand the choices in front of us. When you think about where you're headed with something, what feels right and what feels wrong? Again, are there body clues that suggest that one direction might be better for you than another?

This latter role of sensuality is reminiscent of Jean Piaget's concept of decentration. Piaget was a twentieth-century developmental psychologist responsible for multiple breakthroughs in the field of child psychology. *Decentration* is the term he used for the act of removing yourself from a specific moment in order to consider potential outcomes and possibilities.

In their book, *Piaget or the Advance of Knowledge,* authors Jacques Montanegro and Danielle Maurice-Naville explain the process of decentration:

> A (centered) subject whose perspective is determined by his action has no reason to be conscious of anything other than its results; on the other hand, decentering—that is, displacing one's focus and comparing an action with other possible actions, particularly with those of other people—leads to a consciousness of "how" and to real operations.

Interestingly, while decentration seems to suggest a diminishment of focus, the process aids in focus when the senses are brought into play. When a person first decenters and steps back, if she then allows herself to get a feel for the situation that she is pondering, an increased sense of focus emerges. As we've discussed elsewhere in this book, your senses are providing you with all sorts of information that you might not be paying attention to. When you stop, focus, and allow yourself to listen to your internal signals, you pick up on those things that you're too often missing. You get out of your habits, you pull back from the rush of action, and you consider possibilities that can lead to a level of growth you'll never achieve otherwise.

Not so fast

Stop and Focus is a process that works strongly in the service of your self-story. It's entirely possible that you wouldn't have any sense of your self-story at all if you weren't able to stop and focus on it. Of course, herein lies one of the fundamental problems I'm trying to address with this book: The enormous growth and fulfillment opportunities available through a strongly defined self-story elude far too many people because they believe that stopping and focusing is a luxury they can't afford.

In my work as a consultant, I'm meeting new people all the time, and one of the things that these people tend to bring up very early in our conversations is the speed at which life is moving around them, the sense they get of being overwhelmed by this, and the belief that there is nothing they can do to step away from it.

"Everything is so fast," I've heard more times than I can count. "I'm never offstage. I'm *always on.*" When I suggest that it isn't necessary to be on all the time, a common response is, "I can never stop for two reasons. One is that the guy next to me isn't stopping, and if I don't keep up, I'm out. The other is that the *fast* is not in me—it's in the culture. It doesn't matter what I do."

There are some things wrong with that sentiment. The first

is that always being on all but guarantees that you're not going to be your best and that you're not going to be your truest self. Ultimately, if the goal is to prove your value to your employer, your clients, your colleagues, etc., you're unlikely to do that by being purely reactive, mediocre, and inauthentic. If stopping and focusing allows you a better chance to be great and to be real, that's far preferable to always being on, and you'll do more than catch up when you step back into the stream of action. Having a strong sense of your self-story is an important part of this, so I do understand that there's a certain level of chicken-or-egg here. When you are truly aware of what you are about, you tend to be more comfortable with allowing the world to go on without you for brief stretches while you give yourself a chance to focus.

Another thing wrong with this much-decried notion is that blaming the culture for anything suggests that you as an individual have no effect on the culture. Take that out to its most absurd extreme. If no individual affected the culture in any way, there would be no culture. At a more workable level, there's always something you can do to tweak your environment, even if it is only a little bit. Consider what Troy Wolverton discovered on the trip we discussed at the beginning of this chapter. Not only did he survive going off the grid temporarily; he found the experience edifying and rewarding.

If you really understand what you're about, you're much more likely to feel comfortable letting the world pass you by every now and then in exchange for some time of undeterred contemplation. This is because knowing what you're about gives you a better sense of where you stand. Can you cut out on the monthly product review meeting so you can think more about the future of the product? Probably not, unless your self-story revolves around being unpredictable and unreliable. But can you leave your phone in your desk for an hour at lunchtime to ponder the future? Almost certainly.

chapter nine

Riff on the World

WYNTON MARSALIS IS perhaps the most popular jazz musician in the world. He's won nine Grammys and was the first person to win awards in the jazz and classical categories in the same year (a feat he repeated the following year). He's a recipient of the National Medal of Arts, and he was even the first jazz musician ever to win the Pulitzer Prize for music.

What has always impressed me about Marsalis is his prodigious creativity, which expresses itself both in his formal songwriting and arrangements and in the colors and textures he brings to his spontaneous performances onstage. Because he's one of the planet's great improvisers, it isn't surprising that he sees the opportunity for improvisation everywhere.

"We all improvise," he told me. "Everyone who speaks improvises. On the most fundamental level, improvisation is the way that we live. We improvise in so many ways every day;

we have set patterns—put on the pants . . . pants, shirt, belt. So it's a different shirt, different pants, different belt. Put on your eyeglasses, brush your teeth at certain times. Sometimes it's a different time. Eat different food. Make different choices, use different routes, go on the same route, visiting people you never visited before. Talk to people when you know you're going to have an unpleasant conversation, talk to people you have a sweet conversation with. Go to your friend you've always spoken to. Talk to somebody you've never spoken with. Learn some things, ask questions, provide information, argue with people in the barbershop, call people in your family, relive prior bad experiences. Relive good experiences. Clown, joke around, make up things, put different ideas together where you've never put them together."

To Marsalis, while the chance to improvise is always there, you need to build it upon a foundation. Good improvisation isn't plucked from thin air; it comes from a combination of knowledge and imagination.

"Knowledge is something you've acquired. Imagination is something that you have. It's given to you. How can I transform my knowledge of basketball into dunking? I can't. You can study trumpet all your life; it's not going to make you hit a note like Louis Armstrong. But if *he* hadn't studied it, he wouldn't have hit those notes. But because you study doesn't mean you can hit the notes. Imagination is your thing. We all have it. Every person on earth has that. In jazz, you play and you listen at the same time. So you don't have to be quiet to be listening. But you do have to demonstrate that you're hearing, and that's reflected in the way that you play. We all function from what we know, what we experience and feel. We also feel different things and know different things and we all want to make different things real. That's the beauty."

Marsalis thinks a great deal about the creative process, and he has a distinctive perspective on it, particularly regarding its relationship to improvisation.

"In improvisation, your creativity comes from different sources. One is everything that's around you—what you hear, your contemporaries. You will be like all of them because you are all the same. Everyone in my neighborhood spoke a certain way, wore a certain type of clothes, played a certain style of music, listened to a certain kind of music. Everyone in the same neighborhood at the same time who lived in Cádiz did something different. Everybody who lived in Juárez did something different from that. Everyone who lived in São Paulo did something different from that. But they were all the same and we were all the same.

"That generally extends back into time. It's like the history of an art form. Beethoven says, 'Let me see how Bach executed these fugues; I think I'll write a fugue.' He writes it in his style, but it's a fugue that Bach executed. You might meet a painter and that painter might say, 'Hey, did you ever think about this?' Or you may meet a person who was a housekeeper who's going to say, 'This piece is too long. Did you ever think about . . . ?' That's an artistic sentiment."

What Wynton Marsalis is getting at here is that inspiration leads to inspiration, and genius often builds on the genius that came before it. What we perceive as movements often derive from a particular context and an interpretation within that context that leads to true originality. It became obvious to me as we continued to talk that Marsalis takes this philosophy far beyond music. We went on to discuss his background a bit, and it registered that he has always been his own person.

"I always felt like I had my own kind of thing. I knew guys would ask me what I thought. I knew that if they were fighting, I was not going to be the one who got beat up. I knew that if something happened, they would ask me what I thought. Older guys: 'Man, what you think we should do about this?' Street-level, kind of. I knew I could figure things out. I don't know why. I just knew older people liked me. They liked to talk to me. They would tell me stuff. I don't know why they did it, but I knew that they did it. I knew if I sat in the bar . . . I was in bars and clubs with my daddy. The older guys would always talk to me and they always treated me like I was the mascot. They liked me. 'Yeah, man, Ellis, why don't you bring Wynton back in here, man?' I was, like, their man, and I'm six, seven, eight, nine—you know, young. I just knew like that."

Wynton Marsalis is one of the most *alive* people I've ever met. We've had a number of conversations in different venues, and I've come to see that he is utterly connected to the life that he's living. To him, every conversation, every interaction, every moment with his instrument is an opportunity to celebrate possibility.

He is an extraordinarily accomplished human being. He has done things that most of us will never come close to doing. However, one of the ways in which he has done these things is by mastering a process that is available to all of us, something I call Riff on the World.

Serendipity was my tour guide, assisted by caprice.

—Pico Iyer

The marriage of play and expertise

In jazz music, a riff is a musical phrase or series of phrases that serves as the backdrop for improvisation; in rock music, a riff is often the work of a soloist. When a comedian riffs, it means that he's going off on an extended humorous piece that might take him quite far from the original topic. In storytelling, a riff is a variation on a time-honored theme.

In every case, riffing is about building upon something creatively to come up with something new. It's about using the known as a foundation for exploration. It's about taking the opportunity to participate in variety while honoring some kind of structure. Riffing on the world, then, is about taking the chances life offers you to improvise and to extend yourself beyond where you are today.

Riffing on the world is not about noodling around, about randomly trying new things. I see it as a marriage of play and expertise. Yes, you want to experiment and see how things might turn out, but real riffing is about doing so with some structure behind it. As Wynton Marsalis says, true creativity comes as a combination of imagination and knowledge. All great improvisers know that they can only improvise effectively if they have an intimate understanding of what they're improvising *from*.

The process I'm talking about here is a function of building upon what you know to go further than you've gone before. It's about taking your talents and skills to the next level. Do people rave about your muffins and cookies? Maybe it's time to try baking that multitiered birthday cake. Do you like teaching your kid how to hit a baseball? Maybe it's time to coach a local recreational league team. Does your supervisor regularly credit your contributions to projects? Maybe it's time to pitch an original project to her. Riffing on the world is about considering the things that you're good at and imagining ways in which you can extend that expertise to make your experience more fulfilling.

As with musicians and comedians, there's a certain performance aspect to riffing on the world. Certainly, it's possible to riff alone, but riffing is often most satisfying and exciting when you're doing it in front of an audience. It's a way of showing that you know something so well that you can perform variations on it at the drop of a hat. Yes, it's a form of showing off, but it's also a way to keep your skills sharp and refined.

I'm asked to speak in public regularly. In preparation for these speeches, I will often spend a great deal of time writing a speech and preparing a PowerPoint deck to go along with it. However, when I stand in front of an audience, I find that I rarely deliver the speech that I wrote. Instead, I riff on it. I'll pull facts, references, and quotations from the material I prepared, but the words I use and the paths I go down might be dramatically different from what I planned. I feel comfortable doing this because I know that I've done my homework and that I'm fluent in the topic about which I'm speaking; I have the necessary structure. I also know that I'm likely to perform at a much higher level if I'm being extemporaneous. The theatricality of riffing energizes me and keeps me on edge in a good way.

There's something equally valuable about riffing in that there's a certain amount of risk attached to it. When a comedian starts ad-libbing, there's always the chance that his riff won't be funny. When I go onstage without my script, there's always the chance that I'll be boring. That's scary, and I know I feel a little twinge every time I speak, but it's also remarkably energizing. When you know something well and then push yourself to try variations on that thing "without a net," the possibility of failure electrifies you.

The tremendous benefit of this process is twofold. One is that it is a clear path to self-expansion, to building on your self-story. When you're riffing, you're naturally trying things out, pushing your talents, exploring and maybe exceeding your limits. If you're the baker who tries the multitiered birthday cake, it's possible you'll find out that this is out of your league. It's also possible you'll learn that doing a cake like this is an enormous amount of work that requires a refinement of your skills, but that you're capable of working at this level. And just maybe you'll discover that multitiered birthday cakes are only the tip of the iceberg, and that a wedding cake or maybe a cake that looks like Yankee Stadium is something you'd like to try. Riffing allows you to see how far you're capable of going with anything that matters to you.

The other great value of riffing is that it is a celebration. When you're working from a foundation of skills and improvising from that foundation, you feel incredibly alive and in the moment. There's nothing mundane about riffing; it is an active expression of the best of you. Because of this, it is something you should do as often as feasible.

The thing I love most about coming to my studio
every day is the possibility of discovery. It's about
the object and it's about yourself.

—Hank Virgona, artist

Riffing to produce a feast

While riffing is something you will often find yourself doing on
your own, as with music, the experience can be wildly exploratory when done in collaboration with someone else. In the Jan-
uary 2012 issue, *Food & Wine* magazine chronicled a fascinating
bit of riffing between two world-class chefs. René Redzepi runs
Noma, the Copenhagen restaurant often acknowledged as the
greatest in the world. Daniel Patterson runs the acclaimed Coi,
in San Francisco, among other restaurants, and has been named
a *Food & Wine* Best New Chef. The two met at a food conference
and decided that it would be an interesting exercise to try to
create new dishes together from scratch. "Cooking in a home
kitchen, away from the pressures of their restaurants or a chef-
packed event, they wanted to try to better understand their own
creative processes," wrote journalist Peter Meehan in the *Food &
Wine* piece.

Redzepi and Patterson started at a Bay Area farm and then
continued to a farmers market in San Francisco. Back at Patterson's kitchen, they brainstormed for a while and then rolled up
their sleeves and got to work. They discussed unexplored possibilities for ingredients and shared techniques. Patterson, for example, showed Redzepi his method for "poach-scrambling" eggs.
This inspired Redzepi to use the approach to create an entirely

new dish with aged goat cheese and the nasturtium blossoms he'd found on Patterson's property. At the same time, Patterson made a poach-scrambled egg dish with fresh chèvre and rosemary flowers. When they tried the two preparations, they decided that, while each was delicious, they would taste especially good together, so they combined the two.

The riffing continued to cornmeal pancakes, in which they performed variations on a recipe they found on the Internet and topped the results with a sauce Redzepi was originally planning to use on a veal dish much later in the day. After breakfast, they went foraging together, finding wild berries and wood sorrel, and they immediately considered the possibilities.

Over the course of two days, Redzepi and Patterson created twenty new dishes, many of which made it to the magazine's pages, and none of which existed in their minds before the two of them got together. This is the cooking equivalent of Miles Davis and John Coltrane jamming together or Robin Williams and Ricky Gervais trading ad-libbed one-liners on a stage. It's also a testament to the value and pleasures of riffing together. Redzepi and Patterson each have rich imaginations, and the solo riffing they do in their restaurants is legendary. On this day, though, by riffing in tandem, they created a memorable series of meals that neither was likely to have created on his own.

Playing a tune of reinvention

As Wynton Marsalis mentioned earlier in this chapter, great improvisation is built on a foundation. You can only riff at a high level if you have a clear sense of the fundamentals. When thinking about the bigger riffs in your life—directions for your career or your family, for instance—those fundamentals take the form of your self-story. If you understand your self-story well enough, then you will know where your riffs should take you.

This brings to mind the concept of reinvention, something that can always be a vital part of our self-stories, since our narratives are inherently organic. Sometimes, right in the middle of your narrative, you discover the need for a major "plot complication"—one that is completely consistent with what you are about, but that involves new story elements. When I think of notable public cases of reinvention, I think about George Foreman, an Olympic-gold-medal-winning boxer who became the heavyweight champion of the world by knocking out then-undefeated champ Joe Frazier in two rounds. He was known as a brutal puncher, as indicated by his sixty-eight knockouts in eighty-one professional fights. He won the heavyweight title three times, the third time at age forty-five, which made him the oldest heavyweight champ ever.

There's a fairly good chance, though, that you don't even know that George Foreman was a boxer. Instead, you might think of him only as the spokesperson for the small appliances that bear his name. This is because of a dramatic case of reinvention that might have made little sense from the outside but obviously made tremendous sense to Foreman. What he knew was that inside the surly exterior that he projected during his boxing days, there resided an affable and extremely likable man. This fundamental part of his self-story came to the surface as he became an ordained minister. And when the opportunity came to perform a riff on that story by becoming the face behind a household product, he understood that it was the right riff to play. To underscore the point here, this involved a huge change in his circumstances, but *no* change in the fundamentals of who he was. Everything he needed to reinvent himself was already a central part of who he was and only needed some new packaging. That, to me, is the essential formula in reinvention.

There's no arguing that the formula worked in Foreman's case. The George Foreman line of grills is a gigantically successful product line that has earned Foreman considerably more money and notoriety than he ever received as a fighter. Yet if Foreman hadn't been willing to consider riffing, or if he didn't have enough awareness of his self-story to identify the possibility of this riff, he might have missed this opportunity completely.

Your self-story might suggest riffs for you that you have never considered. Are there paths suggested by what you are about that you haven't yet conceived of taking? Are there elements to who you are that, as with Foreman, have been dormant because they don't fit your current circumstances? Maybe it's time to play a riff or two with one of these.

Riffing: the gift that keeps giving

One of the tremendous side benefits to incorporating the process of riffing into your life is that it prepares you to use it as opportunities arise that require skills you didn't anticipate needing or didn't even necessarily know you had. In a June 2012 article in the *Harvard Business Review*, Michael D. Watkins talks about how people often stumble when they shift from leading a function to leading a much larger enterprise:

What I found is that to make the transition success-
fully, executives must navigate a tricky set of changes in
their leadership focus and skills, which I call the seven
seismic shifts. They must learn to move from specialist
to generalist, analyst to integrator, tactician to strategist, bricklayer to architect, problem solver to agenda set-
ter, warrior to diplomat, and supporting cast member to
lead role.

What caught my eye about this is that many of the transi-
tions Watkins identifies involve the use of skills the potential
leader already has but has not used for this purpose before. For
example, in moving from tactician to strategist, Watkins says it
is essential that the leader "shift fluidly between the details and
the larger picture, perceive important patterns in complex environments, and anticipate and influence the reactions of key external players." In all likelihood, anyone chosen to move on to
the management track has already exhibited the ability to see
beyond the minutiae. Individuals usually need to show a talent
for fitting their functions into the operation as a whole before
they gain candidacy for leadership spots. Where they stumble,
then, is in their lack of facility with riffing. They don't see how to
use the skills that have already worked so well for them against a
bigger corporate backdrop. To go back to the music metaphor,
they don't realize that the virtuosity they learned while playing
bebop can be applied to any jazz style a band might throw at
them. They therefore either feel under-qualified, or they try to
use their old processes without modification, even when those
processes are incompatible with a larger system.

Making riffing a central exercise in your life can shorten the learning curve on any new venture dramatically. If you know how to riff, you know how to bring your talents to any situation that might demand them. Riffing, then, makes not only your current situation more interesting and successful but also other opportunities that show up in your future.

Playing a riff on "and"

Paradox plays a key role in riffing. As we've discussed elsewhere, paradox allows you to look at things not from an either/or perspective but from the viewpoint of "and." The notion of "and" makes available a vast array of options and therefore facilitates your ability to riff on the world.

Roger Martin is the former dean of the University of Toronto's Rotman School of Management, the director of a global strategy consulting firm, and the author of several books. In *The Opposable Mind*, he talks about how an extensive study of great business leaders helped him to discover a key similarity between them:

> I have spent the past fifteen years, first as a management consultant and then as the dean of a business school, studying leaders who have striking and exemplary success records, trying to discern a shared theme running through their successes. Over the past six years, I have interviewed more than fifty such leaders—some for as long as eight hours—and as I listened, a common theme has emerged with striking clarity.

The leaders I have studied share at least one trait, aside from their talent for innovation and long-term business success. They have the predisposition and the capacity to hold two diametrically opposing ideas in their heads. And then, without panicking or simply settling for one alternative or the other, they're able to produce a synthesis that is superior to either opposing idea. Integrative Thinking is my term for this process—or more precisely this discipline of consideration and synthesis—that is the hallmark of exceptional businesses and the people who run them.

Martin wrote of these leaders in an article for the *Huffington Post*, "When faced with an apparent choice between conflicting models or options—each of which bears problematic shortcomings—rather than choose the 'least-worst' option, they utilize the tension of the opposing models to forge a creative resolution in the form of a new model that contains elements of the individual models but is superior to each."

He is, of course, talking about using paradox to riff. And while their riffing might involve decisions regarding tens and even hundreds of millions of dollars, their success underscores the benefit of engaging paradox, and it is applicable even if you're operating on a considerably smaller scale. As you riff on the world, remember to employ your "opposable mind" to do so. Consider the conventional way you approach something and then see what happens when you incorporate components of an opposite approach. At the very least, it will provide you with valuable contrast. However, it's entirely possible that it will give you something much more satisfying: a breakthrough.

Your work is to keep cranking the flywheel that
turns the gears that spin the belt in the engine of
belief that keeps you and your desk in midair.

—Annie Dillard

Sensing an inspired variation

Sensuality's contribution to riffing on the world is in the service
of providing clues. One of the things you'll notice when you
watch two rock guitarists riffing together is that they feed off
each other. Their senses are on high alert while this is happening. They're listening, of course, to what the other guitarist is
playing, and complementing or contrasting whatever it is depending on where their inspiration takes them. They're also
watching, though. One of the things that you'll notice when you
see a great jam is that the musicians are rarely facing away from
each other. They watch each other play to pick up signs about
where the improvisation is going.

I've never played guitar onstage (or anywhere else, for that
matter) with Eric Clapton, Dickey Betts, Trey Anastasio, or any of
the other great improvisational rock guitarists. The closest I come
to this kind of riffing is in a decidedly different setting, when I'm
running a focus group. I know that many people run focus groups
using scripts, bullet points, and prepared questions. I've never
been able to do that, nor am I even interested in doing that. Instead, I approach these groups with a goal in mind—I know what
my client is hoping to learn—but I have no predetermined approach to reaching that goal. Instead, I riff, relying on sensuality.

When my senses are on full alert, I can pick up signals about where the conversation is headed and where it needs to go. Observing body language, I can tell when participants feel engaged in a line of questioning and when they are bored. By listening to vocal intonations, I can tell if a respondent is willing to dig deeper or just dig in his heels. Rooms even feel different when a discussion is leading toward a valuable set of observations.

All of your senses can contribute to your riffing. Obviously, taste and smell had much to do with the riffing that René Redzepi and Daniel Patterson did together, and these can surely contribute to yours as well. The key is setting your senses outward for clues to where you should go with whatever you choose to riff on. If you do, you'll notice that ideas and stimulation can come from surprising sources, and that your riffing will take on added dimension.

Curiosity helps you make the jump

Curiosity is a fundamental resource for exploring where a riff might take you. When your curiosity is engaged in the process of Riff on the World, you see opportunities for riffs in a tremendous number of places. Curiosity lets you imagine outcomes and select options from the wide variety available. Not every riff is worth playing, but many are at least worth exploring. When you're curious, you find potential riffs everywhere.

Igor and Marko Pusenjak were high schoolers in Croatia when they started using the simple programming language of BASIC and the much more complex assembler language to experiment with video game development. College and careers followed, but their joint fascination with games and gaming never waned, even when they moved to different cities. In the meantime, Apple was rolling out the iPhone and introducing a huge consumer base to the enormous new diversion of apps. The Pusenjaks' curiosity kicked into overdrive as they imagined the creative possibilities they could bring to the smartphone world.

Working largely through e-mail, the brothers started riffing on ideas for games they could create using the iPhone's programming platform. They started with an app called Bubblewrap, playing off the seemingly universal fascination with popping the bubbles in the ubiquitous packing material. They came up with a tic-tac-toe app that got a distinctive look from Igor's design training. Then came Eat, Bunny, Eat! another cleverly designed game involving steering a digital rabbit toward falling digital carrots.

It was after Eat, Bunny, Eat! that the Pusenjaks' curiosity took their riffing—and their market reach—to the next level. Eat, Bunny, Eat! had been popular, so it made sense to create a sequel, but Igor couldn't come up with a design that excited him. They decided to explore the creation of a follow-up app from a different direction, and Igor started pencil-sketching new characters. One of them was a green, snouted creature that Igor named the Doodle. This turned out to be an inspired riff, and the brothers decided to play it out. Things took off from there, and before long, Doodle Jump, one of the most popular iPhone apps ever, was a reality. Doodle Jump has been downloaded more than five million times, and it has become a pop culture icon, appearing in sitcoms, showing up onstage during rock concerts, and being buzzed on talk shows. The Pusenjaks have created numerous variations on the game, including ones for Christmas, Easter, and winter, and even one involving characters from Pocket God, another tremendously popular game.

Riffing driven by curiosity is at the heart of their success. From their days in Croatia working on a ZX Spectrum 48K to their early app experimentation to their regular updating of Doodle Jump, the Pusenjaks have continuously wondered what was around the corner, and then built on their themes the way a great jazz saxophonist might.

Certainly there are plenty of people who choose to riff with the same instruments as the Pusenjaks. As of mid-September 2012, close to a million apps had appeared in Apple's App Store, created by nearly two hundred thousand publishers. However, using curiosity in the process of Riff on the World is hardly limited to this particular creative pursuit. A multitude of riffs is available to you simply by turning your curiosity toward things you care about. What are the projects you love most? About which of your accomplishments are you proudest? Have you ever been curious about how you could take these things further, what might happen if you attempted a variation you may not have considered before? Letting your curiosity fly could lead to some inspired new riffs.

Picking up on everything

If curiosity allows you to discover ways in which the things you do might lead to new riffs, openness allows you to create conditions that let the riffs come to you. Riffing is often driven by directed serendipity in that it typically involves traveling down a particular path and seeing which opportunities arise. This could include anything from going to a chamber of commerce meeting to seek spontaneous networking opportunities to riding your bike through the local park looking for a fragment of an idea that might lead to a breakthrough in the project you've been working on.

Or you could use openness in the service of riffing the way Joel Hodgson has. In the late eighties, Hodgson created one of the first hits for the fledgling Comedy Central cable television network when he launched *Mystery Science Theater 3000*. The show had a preposterous premise. Here's the description from IMDb:

> In the not too distant future, a man and his robots are trapped on the Satellite of Love, where evil scientists force them to sit through the worst movies ever made.

As I said, preposterous. However, from this foundation emerged a cult favorite. The reason for the success was riffing. Each episode of *Mystery Science Theater 3000* (known to fans as MST3K) was played out while the man, Joel Robinson (played by Hodgson), and his robots, Tom Servo and Crow, watched a film, commenting throughout on anything and everything that came to mind. For instance:

> (Over a scene of a werewolf driving a car into oil barrels and setting off an explosion)

Servo: So his plan is to rid the world of security guards by changing them into werewolves one by one and having them crash their cars?

Joel: Well, it seems to be working so far. Can't fault him on that.

(During an alien attack of a women's college dormitory)

Joel: Don't even know what panties are, yet they feel compelled to raid.

Crow: Every male of every species has the biological urge to panty-raid.

(During an awkward love scene in a horror movie)

"I've got a mantis in my pantis."

Since viewers weren't interested in the movies themselves (the producers were especially adept at picking the worst of the worst), Hodgson and his small team of writers needed to come up with more than six hundred quips per ninety-minute episode to keep fans engaged. Riffing at this level requires a tremendous degree of openness, and everything was mined for its potential humor. Opening credits, theme music, costumes, props, scenery, hairstyles, and even cultural ephemera served as source material. "When movie riffing is your job," Hodgson said during an interview with Slashdot, "you have to build places into the creative process where you can be loose and say whatever comes to mind. The riffs we made were all products of several passes at improvising to a movie. This usually happens in the writing room. You take the best and shape those into the show."

Through *Mystery Science Theater 3000*, Hodgson created the comedy style known as "movie riffing." It has a limited number of practitioners, but they tend to be especially passionate about the pursuit. Enthusiasm for the form is so high in some circles that Hodgson even started Riff Camp to help students become expert movie riffers. He remains committed to the form on multiple levels. Though he left MST3K in 1993 (it ran until 1999), he still finds movie riffing exciting. In 2007, he launched *Cinematic Titanic*, a live movie riffing show, with several of his fellow *Mystery Science Theater 3000* writers.

Movie riffing is an extreme sport, not one that most of us have the constitution for. However, it provides a sterling example of how one might riff on the world if one is open. What might your version of this be? What would come to you if you allowed yourself to dive deep into your favorite pursuit solely for the purpose of discovering what ideas might pop into your head? What interesting, uncharted pathways might become available to you if you leave yourself open to them?

Your story comes to life when you add a few riffs

The process of Riff on the World performs an invaluable service to your self-story: It offers you a way to see the most delightful of variations. As I mentioned earlier in this chapter when discussing reinvention, and as we saw with people like George Foreman and the Pusenjaks, your self-story can expand and gain true definition when you attempt variations upon the solid foundation of who you are. This is an extremely important point if you want to accomplish everything that you're capable of accomplishing. If you want to make the most of yourself, you need to make a habit of considering ways in which you might evolve the you that already exists, and that very often means playing a riff.

Riffing in its many forms may prove to be extremely productive and fulfilling for you. Beyond anything else, though, it will almost certainly fill your life with more joy and adventure. When you're riffing, you are as "on" as you're likely to get, and when you're "on," you are the most you—and that's a very good thing. I'll let Wynton Marsalis have the last word on this:

"Improvisation gives you an opportunity to displace. Mastery in the spur of the moment is unbelievable."

chapter ten

Vitalize

F RANK THOMAS AND Oliver Johnston were the Lucy and
Desi and the Butch and Sundance of the animation world.
Ask anyone with a sense of the history of the field to name the
greatest animators, and there's an excellent chance that both
Thomas and Johnston will be on the list. They were two of Disney's legendary Nine Old Men, responsible for a string of feature
films that still inspire a sense of wonder more than half a century
after they appeared—films like *Snow White and the Seven
Dwarfs*, *Pinocchio*, and *The Jungle Book*. The spaghetti scene in
Lady and the Tramp? That was them. The guys who killed Bam-
bi's mother? That was them too, and they've taken some heat
over it. Oscar-winning director Brad Bird even paid tribute to
them in a scene from his film *The Incredibles*.

Frank Thomas and Oliver Johnston were legendary film storytellers. Most significantly, they were a legendary *team*. "The
idea of Frank and Ollie," said Disney supervising animator Glen
Keane in the documentary *Frank and Ollie*, "it's a term that is

thrown around so often that I think that there are those who don't know that Frank and Ollie is not one person, that it's two separate individuals. It just flows: frankandollie."

They had a friendship that started when they met as art students at Stanford University and extended for the remaining sixty-plus years of their lives. Through all of those years, they stayed remarkably close.

"They were rooming in the same house and then eventually had an apartment together," said Thomas's wife, Jeanette, in the film. "When Ollie and Marie married, Frank moved across the hall to a bachelor apartment. Next thing I knew Marie was house-hunting with me and we found a duplex, which we bought. Before that, Ollie, Marie, and Frank had bought property in Flintridge. So we were both planning houses at the same time. That August, we both had babies within a week of each other. Ollie and Frank continued to drive to work and back. This went on and on."

"Frank and I started writing together back in art school and that continued on after we both got into Disney," Johnston noted. "Over the years, we had a lot of time to talk to each other. We learned about what each of us thought and how we approached our problems and what we were weak in and strong in."

Thomas found that proximity brought something additional to their work. "Other fellows would stop at five o'clock and just go home and do something else. We still had twenty minutes to half an hour to forty-five minutes to talk about the picture, what was wrong with it, what it needed, and the scenes that we had coming up. When you finally got to work the next morning, you had a pretty clear idea of what you wanted to do, so I would make a lot of little thumbnails, working out the continuity and the expressions. I'd take it in to Ollie and say, 'Was this what you expected to see? What we talked about?' He'd call out the changes he saw and then I would take it back to my room and work on the scene on that basis."

Johnston elaborated on the symbiotic nature of their working relationship. "I'd take a drawing in to him and he'd make some little scribbles over it. He wouldn't try to make a real fancy drawing; he'd just point out maybe what he thought I was missing, or maybe he would point out what he liked about my drawing which I didn't see. In the end, I'd wind up with a much better drawing. I couldn't have done it by myself."

As close as they were—at the time of Thomas's death in 2004, they still lived next door to each other—their styles were not the same.

"Ollie and I have a very different approach to drawing and animating," Thomas said. "He has a sign up on his desk that says, 'What is the character thinking, and why does he feel that way?' He's very perceptive. If you can answer those two questions, you're way down the road toward getting a scene out of it."

"Frank is very analytical," Johnston added. "He figures everything out, makes notes about everything. He figures it all out completely. He went to more trouble planning out a scene than anyone in the studio ever did."

Still, the results were so seamless that it was difficult for even those closest to them to identify where one left off and the other began. "They were always referred to as 'Frank and Ollie,' and I guess in that I had assumed that Frank took the lead in things," said Theodore Thomas, Frank's youngest son and the writer, producer, and director of *Frank and Ollie*. "In the making of the film, I realized how really symbiotic their relationship is and the extent to which my father, as logical as he is, is inclined to explore ideas endlessly, to try every last variation that you could think of on staging or coming up with an action. Only then would he actually implement it. He's constantly searching for that. I think Ollie, in many ways, was extremely helpful to him in saying, 'No, Frank, that's not it. This is it; this is the core.' I was not aware of the extent to which Ollie would take the lead in helping to focus Frank's efforts. Conversely, Frank was able to give a very logical context to the emotional approach that Ollie was having in terms of saying, 'Well, gee, if you do it this way, this is going to be the end result. Is that what you want to do?' "

The Frank and Ollie story is inspiring on many levels. It is the story of a great bromance. It is the story of the potential of teamwork. It is an ode to loyalty and interdependence. What fascinates me most about this story, though, is how it illustrates the effect people can have on each other when they share their deepest levels of engagement.

"The unique friendship that Frank and Ollie had, there will never be another one like that," said Keane. "There's a verse that means a lot to me in Proverbs: 'Iron sharpens iron, so one man sharpens another.' Through this process of them constantly working with one another, constantly rubbing against one another through the different films they've worked on, different problems, I can still see that that was a process that was still going on when I was there with them. You could see them in the hallway. They were constantly rubbing these ideas across one another's surface because they knew that that was how the best things happened as a team of people."

What Frank and Ollie clearly understood, at a level powerful enough to sustain them decade after decade, was that vital lives are extremely satisfying, and those lives are capable of providing vitality to others. They are the standard-bearers for the fifth of our processes, Vitalize.

Thinking like a shaman

By this point in the book, you've hopefully come to embrace the value of gaining full access to your Essentials and using the processes that combine them most effectively to enhance your self-story. These tools and processes bring you closer to the person you were most meant to be and offer you the best chance of leading a fulfilling and contributory life—a vital life.

This brings us to the last of our five processes, one that equally benefits you and the people who matter to you: Vitalize. When you are living a vital life, you feel more joy in the everyday. You find the potential for surprise around every corner, and you feel an intoxicating combination of control and abandon. People who live vital lives also profoundly affect others. I'm sure you've had many experiences with someone "lighting up a room." These are individuals who raise the energy level of the space they inhabit simply by inhabiting it. A moribund meeting electrifies when this person speaks. A party feels more celebratory when this person is around. Your heart beats a little faster in this person's presence, and you feel a little more engaged and a little sharper. This person has learned how to vitalize, and it's something she does without ever forcing the action or imposing herself.

Frank and Ollie lived vital lives. What they were doing had tremendous meaning to them and gave them huge levels of inspiration and joy. As Ollie said in the documentary about working at Disney, "I found out this was the only place I'd ever want to be." This passion and commitment to what they were doing must have been extremely satisfying. And, as we learn through their story, this energy radiated outward. It affected the two of them dramatically. They cajoled each other, drove each other, and coaxed the best out of each other.

They vitalized each other, and they also vitalized those around them. Their excellence and their excitement became an essential part of the Disney animation culture, touching everyone they worked with generation after generation. As *Lion King* art director Andy Gaskill said in *Frank and Ollie*, "It's only in retrospect that I realize the things they were telling us were true secrets of magic."

This, then, is the most satisfying element to the Vitalize process. When you share your vitality with others, you not only make those people feel more alive; you also create the possibility of improving their lives in a permanent way.

I think an inspiring example of this is Lady Gaga. Gaga (real name Stefani Germanotta) exploded onto the world stage in 2008 through her album *The Fame*, her daring videos, and her inventive and uninhibited stage shows. Her albums and songs have sold in massive quantities, which in itself imparts a certain vitalizing force. But Gaga is a rare breed of pop music star whose effect on her followers goes far beyond admiration or idol worship. Her relationship with her fans, whom she calls her Little Monsters, has a foundation in her profound ability to vitalize.

Gaga doesn't simply show her audience a good time; she shows them a way to something better. Her performances, her interviews, her web presence, and her philanthropic work all impart a sense of empowerment to her fans, while the song "Born This Way" celebrates difference and tolerance.

Looking with an anthropologist's eye at the way Gaga affects her audience, I see that she represents an archetype that has been around considerably longer than the *Billboard* Hot 100—the primal, shamanistic high priestess. This is not just because of Lady Gaga's theatrics, wild outfits, headdresses, and masks, although she shares this practice with most shamans, who often paint their faces with natural pigments and dried blood and clothe themselves with feathers from rare birds (or, in Gaga's case, couture made from meat). It's more that these visual and attention-getting means of communication are the necessary accoutrements of the shaman's prototypal ventures out of the temporal, the locally situated familiar, into the "spirit world." Once there, inevitably, the shaman does battle with the dark forces of the cosmos, and as Gaga says, for this you must feel "fierce."

Following the trials of the fight, the shaman comes back to his people (having traveled beyond via trance or hallucinogen) to give to them the lessons—practical, existential, and cosmological—that he has learned. His expertise largely lies in how well these teachings are transmitted, such that the tribe experiences what the shaman experienced, as if they themselves went on the hero's journey. It's a feeling not so much that they participated; instead, they feel a sense of "post-icipation."

This is exactly what Lady Gaga seems to be up to. She is the archetype of the benevolent leader. In an interview with Barbara

Walters, she explained that her goal is to be a teacher to her fans, saying, "I want to liberate them from their fears so they can find their own place in the world." By post-icipating in her journey, each fan feels, "I can become myself." There is no greater gift one can bestow on another. Gaga is artfully full of life so others may be too.

This is how a vital life vitalizes. When you are living your life to the fullest, you naturally generate your vitality for others. However, when you make it your intention—as Frank and Ollie did and as Lady Gaga has—to use your vitality to vitalize others, it not only provides a tremendous service, but it furthers your own sense of fulfillment.

> I found other kids, ninth graders, who also loved
> math and loved having fun.
>
> —Eric Lander, founding director of the Broad Institute of
> Harvard and MIT

Great minds amplify

One way to look at the extraordinary value of this process is to consider what happens when vital lives vitalize each other. This is evident when we consider some of the great teams. John Lennon and Paul McCartney were clearly singular talents in popular music, as their post-sixties work attests. However, when they combined their songwriting genius, the results were eternal. Taking this further, when you include the other team members— George Harrison, Ringo Starr, and producer George Martin—

the combination created arguably the most substantial body of work in pop music history. After the Beatles split, most of the members continued to do exemplary work. Lennon, McCartney, and Harrison are all members of the Rock and Roll Hall of Fame as solo artists, and Martin has been inducted as well. However, their greatness rarely approached what they accomplished consistently as a band.

It's interesting to note that while Lennon and McCartney share songwriting credit on nearly all of their Beatles songs, they rarely wrote together. On occasion, one would contribute a passage to the other's work. A notable example of this is the up-tempo break in "A Day in the Life," a sunnier melody from McCartney that offset Lennon's melancholy in the rest of the tune. With a handful of exceptions, the Lennon-McCartney Beatles songs were either Lennon songs or McCartney songs. Still, these songs are materially different from—and largely superior to—the songs they released in their solo careers. To me, this is clear evidence of vitalizing. Each exerted a force on the other, spurring them to compose at the highest possible level.

Much has been written about the Lennon-McCartney songwriting team and the Beatles. A complete bibliography of Beatles books would probably be longer than this entire volume. Much, much less has been written about an English team from two centuries earlier that illustrates the exponential power of vitalizing.

The Lunar Society of Birmingham started informally in the 1750s with a meeting between Erasmus Darwin and Matthew Boulton. Darwin (grandfather of Charles Darwin) was a doctor and an inventor and had studied at Cambridge University. Boulton had stopped attending school at fourteen, but he had a keen engineering mind. The two found their conversations bracing, and since they both knew geologist John Whitehurst, they invited him to join them, and the three began a wide-ranging correspondence about invention and innovation. The group soon grew to include doctor and mathematician William Small, chemist and glassmaker James Keir, and later potter and industrialist Josiah Wedgwood (founder of the Wedgwood china company), scientist and theologian Joseph Priestley, botanist William Withering, politician and inventor Richard Lovell Edgeworth, author Thomas Day, and physician Jonathan Stokes.

The group was known as the Lunar Society (as were many at the time) because they met for dinner on the Sunday or Monday closest to the full moon. The meetings were informal and largely social, and the group never published their proceedings. However, there is abundant evidence that they exacted a strong positive influence on one another, and for most of them, their greatest work came during the years in which the Lunar Society met. Ten of the fourteen members ultimately became fellows of the Royal Society.

Jenny Uglow wrote a book about this collection of vital individuals titled *The Lunar Men*. She also provided the entry on the Lunar Society of Birmingham for the *Oxford Dictionary of National Biography*. Here, she offers insight into the way the group interacted:

> Lunar interests were kaleidoscopic, ranging from optics and astronomy, chemistry and mechanics, hydraulics and minerals, to meteorology and magnetism, ballooning and ballistics. The practical and theoretical merged. All were

interested in minerals, for example Boulton for metallurgy, Wedgwood for ceramics, Watt, Darwin, Keir, Withering, and Priestley for chemical examination. Boulton, however, exploited the precious Derbyshire fluorite Blue John not for metallurgy, but as bodies for ormolu vases, joining Wedgwood in supplying the taste for classical vases. This movement between aesthetics and scientific research and application typified the society.

She also hints at the vitalizing power the members offered one another in ways that extended far beyond their work:

The members of the Lunar Society passionately believed that their discoveries would make the world a better place. They were the optimistic, and idealistic, forebears of a new class, the nonconformist industrialists and reformers who would dominate nineteenth-century Britain and America. Part of their strength came from their long and deep friendships, providing support in times of trouble. This closeness was reflected by several marriages in later generations, including that of Darwin's son Robert to Wedgwood's daughter Susanna, the parents of Charles Darwin; and of his daughter Violetta to Galton's son Samuel Tertius, the parents of the geneticist Sir Francis Galton.

While it is impossible to quantify the contribution that association with the Lunar Society of Birmingham had on the individuals involved, it is clear that this team of diverse talents and brilliant, curious minds gained inspiration, encouragement, and perspective from their years together. Like Lennon and

McCartney, the Lunar Society brought out the best and most ambitious in one another by the vitalizing force of their intellects, varied perspectives, and common sense of purpose.

These are extreme examples. There will only ever be one Beatles, and history has rarely witnessed a think tank as fertile as the Lunar Society of Birmingham. However, what they show, and what we can share with them, is the remarkable creative power that can be unleashed when we allow ourselves to vitalize.

Pitching your vitality

The process of Vitalize is all about putting yourself out into the world. Self-story—or what you are about—is therefore an indispensable part of this process. As we've discussed elsewhere, your self-story is a nuanced and ever-evolving thing. Projecting the entirety of your self-story outward is not only difficult to do but also absolutely dreadful dinner party conversation. For the purpose of vitalizing, then, there might be something to be learned from the notion of the "elevator pitch."

The elevator pitch comes from the worlds of networking and job hunting, though these days the approach is used for everything from trying to get someone to read your screenplay to speed-dating. The scenario goes something like this: You've just gotten on an elevator alone with someone who could have a tremendously positive influence on your life. You have the length of that elevator ride to convince this person to help you. Your job is to boil down everything that makes your skills or your idea distinctive into a pitch that lasts maybe thirty seconds.

This requires making critical decisions about what you *absolutely need to say*, what can be saved for a follow-up conversation—should your elevator pitch be good enough to generate one—and what is purely window dressing. Elevator pitches are by their nature not comprehensive. They're not even the tip of the iceberg. Rather, a good elevator pitch is like an effective movie trailer—it offers the promise of something substantial and edifying.

In the business world, elevator pitches are valuable ways to get the attention of those who are either tremendously busy or besieged by a large number of people who want to win them over. In terms of vitalizing, the elevator pitch can serve a different but similar function: It can help you to hone your self-story in such a way that it can vitalize others. What part of what you are about do you most want to share with the outside world? How can you get that across with a minimum of words? What most excites you about this that you believe will also excite others?

When thinking about your self-story in this way, keep in mind that you don't actually need to create a pitch. There are plenty of professional and social situations in which such a thing would be unseemly. Imagine, for instance, sitting down with some colleagues and launching into a thirty-second presentation of what makes you so cool. Considering your self-story as an elevator pitch, though, can teach you something about how you project your vitality to others. If you are capable of boiling down the most exciting parts of who you are, it will transfer into the way you carry yourself among others, and you will undoubtedly present yourself with more vitality.

Seeking and sharing vitality

Curiosity plays a central role in vitalizing. It compels you to seek out those who can vitalize you. It also makes you think about when you are at your most vital and compels you to consider how you can share that vitality with others.

Mira Kirshenbaum is the clinical director of the Chestnut Hill Institute and the author of eleven best-selling, award-winning books that have been translated into more than thirty languages. One of those books is *The Emotional Energy Factor*, in which she speaks at length about how to seek out and share vitality.

"Intelligence, generosity, curiosity, all the fine qualities you can imagine are an empty promise without the emotional energy—the enthusiasm, the follow-through, the desire, the hope, the drive, the spark—necessary to bring it to life," she told me. "All the great art in the world, all our wonderful inventions and discoveries, every dream come true—all these would have been impossible without emotional energy. Fatigue, discouragement, frustration are all inevitable every step along the way in life; only emotional energy frees us from their grip."

To her, curiosity extends not only to identifying when you are at your most vital but also to identifying what you need to maintain your emotional energy.

"It's just like vitamins. You don't always need a supplement to give you every vitamin every day. You only need to supplement the vitamins that are missing from your diet. In the same way, you only need to add whatever ingredients are missing to raise your emotional energy. I list twenty-five ingredients of emotional energy in my book *The Emotional Energy Factor*, and I show you how to identify which ones are missing from your life right now. This is valuable because it saves you from adding ingredients of which you already have plenty. Now, if you put a gun to my head and asked me for the one way to raise your emotional energy that most people could benefit most from, I'd say it would be to always do what you really want to do. Putting energy into meeting other people's expectations, into satisfying your less powerful desires, will mean that you will be emotionally starving yourself to death. You only restore your emotional energy when you do what you care about the most."

Kirshenbaum feels that the most telling way to identify whether someone around you has a high level of emotional energy is to see how that person responds to a setback. Those who get on their feet quickly are living vital lives.

Connecting with people of this sort has genuine benefits. "When I'm on a flight and there's bad turbulence, I get uneasy, but I tell myself, 'I'll panic when the flight attendants panic.' Well, as we all go through life, we're all each other's flight attendants. We all give each other signs about whether effort and hope make sense or not. People with high emotional energy convey that yes, it does make sense to keep on keeping on, because they act as though dreams do come true and as though the journey alone is worth the effort. And this is contagious.

"I know a woman who's been having a really tough time finding a job. And yet her emotional energy has generally been high, with the occasional and brief plunge into discouragement. What she does is tell others that she is up and why she is up, without sugarcoating the difficulties. And she tells people what, specifically, she does to keep up her emotional energy. No lecturing or hectoring. She just talks about her own experiences, and that's what others find so inspiring. This is the right way to share your emotional energy. Talk about yourself. People who are down will get the point."

Paying it forward and getting paid back at the same time

Openness has a key role in the process of Vitalize. When you're open, opportunities to share your vitality emerge and, as the members of the Lunar Society learned, this often offers many return benefits.

When you allow yourself to be open to vitalizing, you create the possibility of tremendous growth in others and in yourself, as you benefit in ways that you might not initially imagine. This makes me think of mentoring. Certainly much has been written about the benefits of mentoring with regard to the boost it gives mentees and the soul satisfaction it provides mentors. However, it is entirely possible for a mentor to derive more than just psychic good from the experience.

The Center for Mentoring Excellence is an organization that provides training and tools to individuals and larger operations interested in mentoring. There is a post on the center's site that introduced me to the concept of "reverse mentoring." While there have always been instances of "mentoring up" (playing a mentoring role for your supervisors), more opportunities have arisen because of the digital divide between younger employees and their older bosses.

Thank you for supporting the Homewood Public Library!

Title: Head games
Item ID: 31311005682889
Date due: 6/4/2019,23:59

Title: The 5 essentials :
using your inborn resources
to
Item ID: 31311005103399
Date due: 6/4/2019,23:59

"Reverse mentoring is a fabulous tool for helping a manager or leader learn how younger people are using technology or experiencing a company, and for the younger person to see what is possible for their future," says Dr. Lois Zachary, president of Leadership Development Services, which runs the Center for Mentoring Excellence.

The University of Pennsylvania's Wharton School has a reverse mentoring program in place, in which MBA students work with business leaders all across the country to help them get a better grasp on technology and, indirectly, to get a better feel for the younger generation as both prospective employees and prospective customers.

While such mentoring certainly benefits the older person who might feel overwhelmed by rapidly changing technology, there's a clear advantage to those who provide reverse mentoring. According to Zachary, young people "recognize that reverse mentoring relationships are a huge learning opportunity. The mentee has knowledge that can contribute to the mentor's own professional growth and success."

Clearly, the instances described here go specifically toward a particular exchange of expertise—the younger mentor's innate mapping of the digital landscape and the older mentee's sharing of accumulated business knowledge. However, this serves as an illustration of the win-win potential of consciously working to vitalize others. Offering the vitality of your passions to others is likely to vitalize them, and when charged with this excitement, they are likely to reflect their own vitality back to you, which will bring with it unanticipated rewards.

This all begins with being open enough to seek opportunities to vitalize. Are the things that excite you appropriate for sharing with a community volunteer organization? Are the schools in your area looking for help that you have the expertise to offer? Is there a way to provide a virtual mentorship online? If you allow yourself to be open to the possibilities, you might get back much more than you give out.

> The wiring of the brain at this point in our evolutionary history is such that connections from the emotional systems to the cognitive systems are stronger than connections from the cognitive systems to the emotional systems.
>
> —Joseph LeDoux, *The Emotional Brain*

Your vital brain

Vitalizing has much more to do with sensuality than you might initially imagine. While certainly the process is at heart an emotional one, there's quite a bit going on in our brains when we share our enthusiasm with others.

Rebecca Saxe is a cognitive neuroscientist who runs Saxelab at MIT. When she was a graduate student at the school, she discovered that there is a specific region in our brains that becomes active when we think about others, known as the right temporoparietal junction, or right TPJ. This part of the brain is dedicated exclusively to thinking about the thoughts of others, and has no other role in cognition.

Saxe used the discovery of the right TPJ to embark on a series of experiments to identify the varieties of ways in which people think about the thoughts of others. During her talk at the 2009 TEDGlobal conference, she gave an example of one such experiment. She posed three scenarios involving a woman named Grace and a friend of hers as they tour a chemical factory. During a break Grace goes to get coffee for her friend. In the first scenario, Grace sees a pot that contains sugar but is labeled "deadly poison," puts it in her friend's coffee, and gives it to her friend, who is unharmed because there was no actual poison in the pot. In the second scenario, the pot is labeled "sugar" and contains sugar, Grace makes the coffee, and everything turns out fine. In the third scenario, the pot is labeled "sugar" but actually contains a deadly poison; Grace's friend drinks the coffee and dies.

After the experiment, participants were asked to assess blame. Predictably, they felt that Grace deserved no blame at all for the second scenario, a moderate amount of blame for the third (in which the friend dies), and a great deal of blame for the first (in which the friend is fine, but Grace was clearly trying to kill her). Interestingly, activity in the right TPJ was significantly higher when participants were considering the most nuanced scenario, in which Grace accidentally kills her friend. What this indicates is that we extend our senses outward at a much more intense rate when we find ourselves in situations in which it is important to seriously consider what others might be thinking.

"We have a special brain system that lets us think about what other people are thinking," Saxe said during the talk. "This system takes a long time to develop, slowly throughout the course of childhood and into early adolescence. And even in adulthood, differences in this brain region can explain differences among adults in how we think about and judge other people."

What Saxe shows us is that our senses play a meaningful part in the Vitalize process. When we extend ourselves outward, we are literally turning other people on.

Vitality is no conundrum

I suppose the central paradox in the service of this process is that giving away some of your vitality actually has the effect of generating more vitality within you. This is what Mira Kirshenbaum is referring to when she talks about the contagious qualities of sharing your emotional energy—some of that reflects back to you. This paradox is what reverse mentoring is all about—when you give, you get. It's what the members of the Lunar Society discovered in contributing their ideas and energy to the collective—it had the effect of making their own pursuits more vital. And it is surely what Frank and Ollie learned and what Lennon and McCartney learned as they fed each other energy and fed off each other's energy.

The energizing circle

The effect of this process on your self-story is a profound one. By attempting to be a more vital force in the world, you give yourself a level of definition you might not have had before. Consider the "elevator pitch" exercise we discussed earlier in the chapter. When you begin to think of the parts of what you are about that are most likely to excite and energize others, you find what is most essential about you. I would hope that one of the most exciting things about that exercise would be that you would find it exceedingly difficult to compress all of your finest attributes into such a small space. Equally exciting, though, is that you are likely to find yourself thrilled at the prospect of expressing your vitality to others. This will happen when you have a genuine sense of pride in your self-story. This speaks once again to the cyclical nature of this particular process: In seeking ways to vitalize, you vitalize yourself.

Of all the processes, Vitalize has the potential to have the widest possible effect. That is why I have presented it last. The other processes—Always Be on Your Way Home, Own Your Narrative, Stop and Focus, and Riff on the World—aid you in becoming the most *you* you, in being the person you were truly meant to be. Vitalize assists in this way as well, as you can see from the stories in this chapter, but it also allows you to bring who you are and the joy you feel in being an optimal version of yourself into the world as a whole. That's a tremendously rewarding experience, one that will fill you with the sense of purpose that I hope this entire book has led you to seek. The you that you are truly meant to be is someone you need to be. When you have a vivid and fully realized self-story working for you, you're armed with the kind of fortitude that allows you to stake a place for yourself in the world, overcome hardship better, and simply enjoy life more.

Equally important, though, the you that you are truly meant to be is something that *all* of us need you to be. As this chapter shows, we benefit greatly from the vitality of others. A world with more vital presences is a considerably better world, in which all of us can live.

Afterword

THE GOAL OF this book has been to urge you to experience and participate in your life in the fullest possible way. My hope is that as you have gone through these pages, you've started to take the steps that will allow you to come a little closer to your true nature, and you've begun to use the tools and processes that can make your life more fulfilling and eminently more interesting. Maybe this book has spurred you to consider a career change or a move within your career that will make you feel better about what you're doing. Maybe it has made you think about what your relationships contribute to you and what you contribute to your relationships. Maybe this book has helped you to realize that there are tools at your disposal that you're not using as effectively as you could, and that using them in a better way could have a meaningful effect on your life. Regardless, I hope you now appreciate how having a fully developed self-story and a clear vision of that self-story can lead you to be the best possible version of you. No matter what you want from your life, whether it's vast accomplishment or simply a modicum of satisfaction (or both), you're much more likely to get it if you're utilizing your self-story.

I genuinely believe that making the most of the tools and processes described in this book will enrich your experience and fill you with a greater sense of purpose. However, these tools and processes are not magic spells that will instantly transform you. You have not, simply by reading these pages, become everything you ever wanted to be (I'm guessing this has already occurred to you). You need to engage. I would hope, though, that after reading this book you will have decided that the experience you'll have when you make the Essentials a bigger part of your life is one worth having—that the search for *you* is a search worth embarking upon.

I'd like to suggest that you try something as soon as you close this book. I'd like you to give yourself a few minutes to stop and focus on the following question: What do I want most for myself? Let that question simmer for several minutes, even if an answer leaps instantly to mind. Allow yourself to simply think about it. Then I would like you to ask yourself the following questions based on what you've experienced with this book:

- How can I use my Essential of curiosity to explore possibilities I haven't considered before?
- How can I use my Essential of openness to put myself in situations in which the serendipitous might happen?
- How can I use my Essential of sensuality to experience the conditions that feel most right for me?
- How can I use my Essential of paradox to combine seemingly opposite things to accomplish my goal?

- If this thing I want for myself is genuine, then it is home. How do I point myself in that direction?
- How do I do the things that I'm doing now in new ways that will help me reach my goal?
- How do I create vitality with this endeavor, and whose vitality can I share along the way?

Then, once you've answered these questions, you can ask yourself the most important one:

- How does this thing that I want fit into—and maybe evolve—what I am about?

This might very well be the most important exercise you put yourself through, but only if you do it honestly and with a real desire to expand yourself in a meaningful way. If you allow for the possibility that it will lead to a bigger, more authentic you, then there's the very real chance that it will happen. And make sure to enjoy the process. We're supposed to have fun when we're growing like this.

Again, though, this isn't about a quick fix. The answers you provide yourself here might lead to years of work. In closing, then, I want to leave you with two thoughts, both of which speak to the nuance of this exercise.

The first comes via Werner Herzog's film *Fitzcarraldo*. The film, based on a true story, tells of the attempts of a man, Brian Sweeney Fitzgerald, to pull a 320-ton steamer ship through a patch of jungle to get it from one river to another, where it will be used to transport the rubber that will ultimately fund Fitzgerald's dream of building an opera house in the wilderness. In the end, Fitzgerald doesn't succeed in his quest, but we're left with the image of him playing Caruso from his boat and the sense that his efforts have brought him a real measure of satisfaction. What's most instructive about this ending is that it is not about compromise or about making do with less. It is about how in the process of exploring your goals, your truest goals emerge. By the end of *Fitzcarraldo*, Fitzgerald has evolved his goal. His true goal, which he only learned by embarking on the journey, was to live with his love of opera and boating on the river. At the beginning of the film, he believed that to be the person he wanted to be, he needed the spectacle of building an opera house; by the end, he understood that the spectacle was only a facade.

The second thought comes from David Remnick's extensive profile of Bruce Springsteen in the July 30, 2012 issue of *The New Yorker*. Toward the end of the piece, he quotes Springsteen as saying, "Our effort is to stay with you, period, to have you join us and to allow us to join you for the ride—the *whole* ride. That's what we've been working on the whole time, and this show is the latest installment, and, in many ways, it's the most complicated installment, because in many ways it has to do with the end of that ride. There are kids who are coming to the show who will never have seen the band with Clarence Clemons in it or Danny Federici—people who were in the band for thirty years. So our job is to honor the people who stood on that stage by putting on the best show we've ever put on. To do that, you've got to acknowledge your losses and your defeats as well as your victories. There is a finiteness to it, though the end may be a long time away. We end the night with a party of sorts, but it's not an uncomplicated party. It's a *life* party—that's what we try to deliver up."

This book, then, has been a suggestion to pull your own ship across the jungle, an invitation to your life party. It is an exhortation to truly live. Whether you accomplish your original goals, discover new goals, or discover yourself in the search for your goals isn't the point. The point is that making the most of what you have to work with—and not selling that capacity short—will provide you with more fulfillment, more of a sense of accomplishment, and more fun. Regardless of what you do with what you have inside you, you will be overwhelmingly richer for having used all of your essential resources.

Notes

Chapter One: The Essential of Curiosity

7 **Ever tried:** "Samuel Beckett Quotes," BrainyQuote, http://www
.brainyquote.com/quotes/authors/s/samuel_beckett.html.

9 **We shape our tools:** Ian Austen, "Early Media Prophet Is Now
Getting His Due," *The New York Times*, July 25, 2011, http://www
.nytimes.com/2011/07/26/books/marshall-mcluhan-media
-theorist-is-celebrated.html.

17 **We are stardust:** "We Are Star Dust—Symphony of Science,"
YouTube video, 2:59, posted by "melodysheep," May 9, 2012,
http://www.youtube.com/watch?v=8g4d-rnhuSg.

Chapter Two: The Essential of Openness

24 **Try to remain permanently confused:** George Saunders, *The
Braindead Megaphone* (New York: Riverhead, 2007).

28 **The whole song really is just one sound:** Paul Simon, "The Story
of 'Graceland' as told by Paul Simon," *Graceland 25th Anniversary Edition*, Legacy Recordings, 2012, CD.

29 **People want more space:** David Brooks, "The Talent Society,"
The New York Times, February 21, 2012.

30 **Technology companies sometimes keep the "beta" label:**
Amazon.com review, "Thomas Friedman Interviews Reid
Hoffman and Ben Casnocha," Amazon.com, http://www.amazon
.com/Start-up-You-Future-Yourself-Transform/dp/0307888908/
ref=sr_1_1_title_0_main?s=books.

31 **Whatever you may be thinking:** Thomas L. Friedman, "The
Start-up of You," *The New York Times*, July 12, 2011, http://www
.nytimes.com/2011/07/13/opinion/13friedman.html?_r=1.

31 **It's difficult to argue:** This source was also used for this
passage:
Reid Hoffman and Ben Casnocha, *The Start-up of You: Adapt to
the Future, Invest in Yourself, and Transform Your Career*
(New York: Crown Business, 2012).

32 **I came in with a dream:** Allie Walker, "How to Evolve Creativity
Through Chaos [Need to Know]," PSFK, http://www.psfk.com/
2012/05/need-to-know-nick-barham.html.

33 **The difference between Mr. Gates:** Jim Collins and Morten
T. Hansen, "What's Luck Got to Do with It?" *The New York
Times*, October 29, 2011, http://www.nytimes.com/2011/10/30/
business/luck-is-just-the-spark-for-business-giants.html?_r=1.

35 **In the previous chapter:** The following sources were used for
this passage:
"Early Days," Jane Goodall Institute, http://www.janegoodall.org/
janes-story.
"Jane Goodall Biography," Bio.com, http://www.biography.com/
people/jane-goodall-9542363?page=1.
Robin McKie, "Chimps with Everything: Jane Goodall's 50 Years
in the Jungle," *Observer*, June 26, 2010, http://www.guardian
.co.uk/science/2010/jun/27/jane-goodall-chimps-africa
-interview.
Hans Weise, "From England to the Forests of Africa," Peace
Chain, http://peace-chain.tripod.com/id119.html.

38 **Do you want to tell a story with me:** "TEDxVictoria—Dave
    Morris: The Way of Improvisation," YouTube video, 10:50, posted
    by "TEDxTalks," January 7, 2012, http://www.youtube.com/
    watch?v=MUO-pWJ0riQ.

Chapter Three: The Essential of Sensuality

47 **The words or the language:** Ronald D. Kriz, "Envisioning Scien-
    tific Information: Three Visual Methods: Envisioning Gradients,
    Function Extraction, and Tensor Glyphs," Virginia Polytechnic
    Institute and State University, http://www.sv.vt.edu/classes/
    ESM4714/VizMtd.html.

50 **Dick Fosbury was a flop:** The following sources were used for
    this passage:

    Aimee Berg, "In the Stands with Dick Fosbury," Team USA,
        http://www.teamusa.org/News/2008/August/20/In-the
        -Stands-With-Dick-Fosbury.aspx.

    "Dick Fosbury," *USA Track & Field,* http://www.usatf.org/hallof
        fame/TF/showBio.asp?HOFIDs=57.

    Richard Hoffer, *Something in the Air: American Passion and Defiance
        in the 1968 Mexico City Olympics* (New York: Free Press, 2009).

    "Sports Biographies: Fosbury 'Dick' (Richard D.)," HickokSports
        .com, http://www.hickoksports.com/biograph/fosburydick
        .shtml.

    Jody Zarkos, "Raising the Bar: A Man, the 'Flop' and an Olympic
        Gold Medal," Sun Valley Guide, http://www.svguide.com/
        s04/s04_fosburyflop.htm.

52 **Whenever I think of sensuality:** The following sources were
    used for this passage:

    Dennis Bounds, "Columbo: U.S. Police Drama," Museum of
        Broadcast Communications, http://www.museum.tv/eotv
        section.php?entrycode=columbo.

    "Columbo," Wikiquote, http://en.wikiquote.org/wiki/Columbo.

54 **You don't have relationships:** Mo Rocca, "The Big Conversation," *Arrive*, July/August 2011.

54 **Anna Quindlen, a Pulitzer Prize–winning journalist:** Terry Gross, "Anna Quindlen: Over 50, and Having 'Plenty of Cake,'" *Fresh Air* from WHYY, NPR (April 2012), http://www.npr.org/player/v2/mediaPlayer.html?action=1&t=1&islist=false&id=150738848&m=151274203.

56 **I've always sensed:** Mervyn Rothstein, "Theater: A Novelist Faces His Themes on New Ground," *The New York Times*, December 20, 1987, http://www.nytimes.com/1987/12/20/theater/theater-a-novelist-faces-his-themes-on-new-ground.html?page wanted=all.

Chapter Four: The Essential of Paradox

61 **The Jazz Age was a heady time:** The following sources were used for this passage:
"About: The Chicken & Waffles Story," Dame's Chicken and Waffles, http://www.dameschickenwaffles.com/about.
E. R. Shipp, "Which Came First: The Chicken or the Waffle?" The Root, http://www.theroot.com/views/which-came-first-chicken-or-waffle?page=0,1.

62 **As a writer just beginning:** Stephen Railton, "Introduction," in *Adventures of Huckleberry Finn* (Buffalo, NY: Broadview Press, 2011), 9–38.

65 **Don't take yourself too seriously:** "Bruce Springsteen SXSW Keynote Speech Part 1," YouTube video, 15:00, posted by "jm32coop," March 31, 2012, http://www.youtube.com/watch?v=NYUMcBihPoM.

67 **Where Folds most notably embraces paradox:** Ben Folds, "The Luckiest," *Rockin' the Suburbs*, Epic, 2001, CD.

67 **What Folds appears to have uncovered:** Ben Folds, "Gracie," *Songs for Silverman*, Epic, 2005, CD.

67 **What Folds appears to have uncovered:** Ben Folds, "There's Always Someone Cooler Than You," *Supersunnyspeedgraphic, the Lp*, Epic, 2006, CD; Ben Folds Five, "Evaporated," *Whatever and Ever Amen*, 550 Music, 1997, CD; These sources were also used for this passage:

"Brand New Album!" *PledgeMusic*, http://www.pledgemusic .com/projects/benfoldsfive.

Isabel Braverman, "Ben Folds—'Way to Normal' CD Review," *Imprint Magazine*, October 5, 2008, http://www.imprint magazine.org/music/ben_folds_way_normal_cd_review.

68 **Thinking about paradox:** The following sources were used for this passage:

Louis C.K.: Hilarious, DVD, directed by Louis C.K. (New York: Comedy Central, 2010).

Louis C.K., interview by Jonah Weiner, *Rolling Stone*, December 2011, http://www.jonahweiner.com/RS_Louie_CK_Jonah_ Weiner.html.

Rob Turbovsky, "Louis C.K.: Escape to Reality," Laughspin, http:// www.laughspin.com/2010/06/28/louis-c-k-escape-to-reality/.

Jonah Weiner, "How Louis C.K. Became the Darkest, Funniest Comedian in America," *Rolling Stone*, December 12, 2011, http://www.rollingstone.com/movies/news/how-louis-c-k -became-the-darkest-funniest-comedian-in-america-20111212.

70 **One of Ferran Adrià's stated goals:** The following sources were used for this passage:

"El Bulli: Cooking in Progress," elbullimovie.com, http://www .elbullimovie.com/.

Michael Paterniti, "He Might Be a Prophet. That, or the Greatest Chef in the World," *Esquire*, July 1, 2001, http://www.esquire .com/features/food-drink/ESQ0701-JULY_FERRAN.

Sally L. Steinberg, "Brainstorming the Sweet Potato—El Bulli, the Movie," The Arts Fuse, http://artsfuse.org/39605/brain storming-the-sweet-potato-%E2%80%94-el-bulli-the-movie/.

72 **Part of me suspects:** "John Lennon Quotes," ThinkExist.com, http://thinkexist.com/quotation/part_of_me_suspects_that_ i-m_a_loser-and_the/168683.html.

72 **Even our nervous system:** Laura Freberg, *Discovering Biological Psychology* (Boston: Houghton Mifflin, 2006).

73 **There is no love without aggression:** Konrad Lorenz, *On Aggression* (New York: Harcourt, Brace & World, 1966).

73 **Some paradoxes seem immune to mixing:** John Tierney, "Can a Playground Be Too Safe?" *The New York Times*, July 18, 2011, http://www.nytimes.com/2011/07/19/science/19tierney.html?_r=0.

75 **The resemblance between the process:** Gregory Bateson, *Steps to an Ecology of Mind* (New York: Ballantine, 1972).

76 **What's the most effective platform:** The following sources were used for this passage:
Bridget Foley, "Stella Performance," *W*, October 2007, http://www.wmagazine.com/celebrities/2007/10/stella_mccartney? currentPage=1.
Jess Cartner-Morley, "Stella McCartney: 'Fashion People Are Pretty Heartless,'" *The Guardian*, October 4, 2009, http://www.guardian.co.uk/lifeandstyle/2009/oct/05/stella -mccartney-fashion-heartless.

Chapter Five: The Essential of Self-Story

86 **Schopenhauer, in his splendid essay:** Joseph Campbell, Bill D. Moyers, and Betty S. Flowers, *The Power of Myth* (New York: Anchor, 1991).

87 **Neuroscientist Antonio Damasio:** Antonio R. Damasio, *The Feeling of What Happens: Body and Emotion in the Making of Consciousness* (New York: Harcourt, 2000).

88 **The second part of your self-story:** Arnold Hano, "Can Archie Bunker Give Bigotry a Bad Name?" *The New York Times*, March 12, 1972.

91 **There is a story:** Michael Ondaatje, *The Cat's Table* (New York: Alfred A. Knopf, 2011).

92 **One of the most illuminating components:** The following sources were used for this passage:

"Creation Stories from Around the World," University of Georgia, http://www.gly.uga.edu/railsback/CS/CSIndex.html.

"Links to Creation Myths from Around the World," Magic Tails, http://www.magictails.com/creationlinks.html.

93 **He traced his fascination:** "Bruce Springsteen SXSW Keynote Speech Part 1."

94 **Human personal intuition:** "Academy of Achievement—Steven Spielberg Speech," YouTube video, 11:55, December 18, 2010, www.youtube.com/watch?v=KOJkq7UdIDg.

94 **It is not words:** Ralph Waldo Emerson, *Nature, Addresses, and Lectures* (Boston: Houghton, Mifflin and Company, 1883).

95 **Metaphors are wonderfully supple:** "Albert Einstein Quotes," Albert Einstein Site Online, http://www.alberteinsteinsite.com/ quotes/einsteinquotes.html; Keith Richards and James Fox, *Life* (New York: Back Bay, 2011).

96 **Examine all things intensely:** Annie Dillard, *The Writing Life* (New York: Harper & Row, 1989).

98 **It began with a mental picture:** Jean Stein, "William Faulkner, the Art of Fiction No. 12," *The Paris Review*, http://www.thepar isreview.org/interviews/4954/the-art-of-fiction-no-12-william -faulkner.

98 **I don't always know:** Adam Begley, "Don DeLillo, the Art of Fiction No. 135," *The Paris Review*, http://www.theparisreview.org/ interviews/1887/the-art-of-fiction-no-135-don-delillo.

99 **What I'm perpetually trying to work out:** Barbara Milton, "Margaret Drabble, the Art of Fiction No. 70," *The Paris Review*, http://www.theparisreview.org/interviews/3440/the-art-of -fiction-no-70-margaret-drabble.

100 **There's also much to be learned:** Pam Belluck, "To Tug Hearts, Music First Must Tickle the Neurons," *The New York Times*, April 18, 2011, http://www.nytimes.com/2011/04/19/science/19brain .html?_r=1.

101 **The point that Cash is making here:** The following sources were used for this passage:

"Pete Rose," Baseball-Reference.com, http://www.baseball -reference.com/players/r/rosepe01.shtml.

"Pete Rose," ESPN, http://espn.go.com/mlb/player/bio/_/id/397/ pete-rose.

102 **Nobuyuki Tsujii is the first blind pianist:** The following sources were used for this passage:

Donald Munro, "The Beehive Interview: Nobuyuki Tsujii," Fresnobeehive.com, http://fresnobeehive.com/?s=Nobuyuki+ Tsujii.

"Nobuyuki Tsujii Live at Carnegie Hall," Presto Classical, http:// www.prestoclassical.co.uk/r/EuroArts/2059088.

"Nobuyuki Tsujii, Piano Gold Medal Joint Winner of the 2009 Van Cliburn Piano Competition," Carmel Music Society, http://www.carmelmusic.org/concerts_2011-12/2011 -2012-01/index.html.

103 **"Early on,":** Barbara Ellen, "Danny DeVito: 'It All Worked Out for Me. Life Is Good,'" *The Observer*, April 14, 2012, http://www.guard ian.co.uk/film/2012/apr/15/danny-devito-interview-sunshine-boys.

104 **Know your own bone:** "Henry David Thoreau," PBS, http://www .pbs.org/wgbh/amex/brown/peopleevents/pande04.html.

104 **As human beings:** Jason Gots, "Your Storytelling Brain," Big Think, http://bigthink.com/think-tank/your-storytelling-brain.

Chapter Six: Always Be on Your Way Home

111 **Chuck Jones was the multi-award-winning animator:** The following sources were used for this passage:

"About Chuck Jones," Chuck Jones, http://chuckjones.server700
.com/chuck-jones/biography/.

Paul Bacon, Greg Ford, and Margaret Selby, "Chuck Jones: Extremes and In-Betweens—A Life in Animation," *Great Performances*, directed by Margaret Selby (PBS, 2009).

"Chuck Jones," Academy of Achievement, http://www.achievement
.org/autodoc/page/jon1bio-1.

Chuck Jones: Memories of Childhood, directed by Peggy Stern
(New York: Gladeyes Films, 2009)."Quotes by Chuck Jones,"
Chuck Jones, http://chuckjones.server700.com/chuck-jones/
quotes-by-chuck-jones/.

"Quotes by Chuck Jones," Chuck Jones, http://chuckjones
.server700.com/chuck-jones/quotes-by-chuck-jones/.

114 **I believe that the fundamental experiences:** Andrew O'Hagan,
"Norman Mailer, the Art of Fiction No. 193," *The Paris Review*,
http://www.theparisreview.org/interviews/5775/the-art-of-fiction
-no-193-norman-mailer.

119 **I think there's an interesting model:** The following sources
were used for this passage:

"Encyclopedia Playoff Edition: Jerry West," NBA.com, http://
www.nba.com/history/players/west_bio.html.

"History of the Lakers," NBA.com, http://www.nba.com/lakers/
history/lakers_history_new.html.

120 **We live in linear time:** Jeanette Winterson, "Behind the Masks,"
The New York Times, May 16, 2012, http://www.nytimes
.com/2012/05/13/books/review/in-one-person-by-john-irving
.html?pagewanted=all&_r=0.

122 **There are also strong traditions related to gender:** "Breaking
Traditions Award 2007," Missouri Center for Career Education,
http://www.missouricareereducation.org/project/btaward/
bt2007.php.

123 **Consider television journalist Steve Hartman:** The following
sources were used for this passage:

"Steve Hartman," CBSNews, April 4, 2012, http://www.cbsnews
.com/8301-18564_162-509349/steve-hartman/.

Steve Hartman, "Everybody in the World Has a Story, Round 2,"
Couric & Co. (blog), *CBS Evening News*, September 13, 2010,
http://www.cbsnews.com/8301-500803_162-20016308
-500803.html?tag=contentMain;contentBody.

Steve Hartman, "Meet Steve Hartman's Human GPS," CBSNews,
November 6, 2010, http://www.cbsnews.com/2100-500617
_162-6970021.html.

125 **Sensuality can also offer you your first steps:** "About the Symphony of Science," Symphony of Science, http://symphonyofscience
.com/about.html.

127 **Frank Jacobs has found:** The following sources were used for
this passage:

Frank Jacobs and Sarah Duguid, "First Person: Frank Jacobs," *FT
Magazine*, March 25, 2011, http://www.ft.com/cms/s/2/
18bddb2c-54f0-11e0-96f3-00144feab49a.html.

Staff, "You Can't Get There from Here," *Utne Reader*, July–
August 2010, http://www.utne.com/Arts-Culture/Strange
-Maps.aspx.

"Strange Maps Posts," Big Think, http://bigthink.com/blogs/
strange-maps.

129 **A useful way of illustrating this:** The following sources were
used for this passage:

David Dye, "Ray LaMontagne: From Left Field to Center Stage,"
World Cafe, NPR, October 9, 2006.

Nicole Perlroth and Isabelle Schafer, "Celebrity Career-
Changers," *Forbes*, March 25, 2010, http://www.forbes.com/
2010/03/25/sarah-palin-television-leadership-second-acts
-celebrities.html.

"Ray LaMontagne," AllMusic, http://www.allmusic.com/artist/
ray-lamontagne-mn0000182302.

Ellen Sterling, "Ray LaMontagne: Digging Deep and Doing What He Does," *The Blog* (blog), Huffington Post, September 2, 2010, http://www.huffingtonpost.com/ellen-sterling/ray-lamontagne-digging-de_b_703077.html.

Chapter Seven: Own Your Narrative

131 **Michael Lee is the founder:** The following sources were used for this passage:

"About Us," Phoenix Rising Yoga Therapy, http://www.pryt.com/history-of-pryt/.

Michael Lee, "The Birth and Development of Phoenix Rising," Phoenix Rising Yoga Therapy, pryt.com/content/uploads/2012/09/LTW2011PRYTBirth.pdf.

142 **One of the most extreme ways:** "The Vision Quest," Rites of Passage, http://www.ritesofpassagevisionquest.org/the-vision-quest.html.

145 **I awoke from one of those truncated sleeps:** Bob Livingstone, *The Body Mind Soul Solution: Healing Emotional Pain Through Exercise* (New York: Pegasus, 2007).

149 **Bryant Austin had been a wildlife photographer:** The following sources were used for this passage:

Yudhijit Bhattacharjee, "Whales' Grandeur and Grace, Up Close," *The New York Times*, April 18, 2011, http://www.nytimes.com/2011/04/19/science/19profile.html?_r=1.

Jaymi Heimbuch, "Ocean Film Fest 2010—Bryant Austin Creates World's First Life-Sized High Res Photos of Whales," Tree-Hugger, http://www.treehugger.com/natural-sciences/ocean-film-fest-2010-bryant-austin-creates-worlds-first-life-sized-high-res-photos-of-whales.html.

Zoe J. Sheldon, "Whale Tales: Bryant Austin's Life-Sized Portraits," Sierra, http://sierraclub.typepad.com/greenlife/2011/05/tales-of-a-whale-bryant-austins-life-sized-portraits.html.

Chapter Eight: Stop and Focus

153 **Even today:** Troy Wolverton, "Wolverton: Going Off the Grid—
and Loving It," MercuryNews.com, August 26, 2012, http://www
.mercurynews.com/troy-wolverton/ci_21386413/wolverton
-going-off-grid-and-loving-it.

156 **He who can no longer:** "Albert Einstein Quotes," ThinkExist
.com, http://thinkexist.com/quotation/the_most_beautiful_
thing_we_can_experience_is_the/12647.html.

159 **Sometimes you need:** "Sebastian Vettel," BrainyQuote,
http://www.brainyquote.com/quotes/quotes/s/sebastianv417864
.html.

159 **Distractions come in numerous forms:** The following sources
were used for this passage:
Henry Abbott, "The Lakers' Mental Preparation for Game 7,"
ESPN, http://espn.go.com/blog/truehoop/post/_/id/16803/
the-lakers-mental-preparation-for-game-7.
Jordan Gaines, "Head-to-Head Competition: It Really Is Mind
Over Matter," *Brain Babble* (blog), *Psychology Today*, September 7, 2012, http://www.psychologytoday.com/blog/
brain-babble/201209/head-head-
competition-it-really-is-mind-over-matter.
Simon Hartley, "Athletic Focus and Sport Psychology: Key to
Peak Performance," *Podium Sports Journal*, http://www
.podiumsportsjournal.com/2010/12/09/athletic-focus-sport
-psychology-key-to-peak-performance/.

165 **Here's where paradox comes in:** The following sources were
used for this passage:
Elizabeth Reninger, "Wu Wei: The Action of Non-Action," About
.com, http://taoism.about.com/od/wuwei/a/wuwei.htm.
"What Is Nondoing?" Lao Tzu and Tao Te Ching, http://taoisminfo
.com/nondoing.html.

168   **A (centered) subject:** Jacques Montangero and Danielle
      Maurice-Naville, *Piaget or the Advance of Knowledge* (Mahwah,
      NJ: L. Erlbaum Associates, 1997).

Chapter Nine: Riff on the World

173   **Wynton Marsalis is perhaps:** "Biography," Wynton Marsalis
      Enterprises, http://wyntonmarsalis.org/about/bio.

177   **Serendipty was my tour guide:** Liesl Schillinger, "Pico Iyer's Kin-
      ship with Graham Greene," *The New York Times*, December 30,
      2011, http://www.nytimes.com/2012/01/01/books/review/the-man
      -within-my-head-by-pico-iyer-book-review.html?pagewanted=all.

177   **In jazz music:** "riff," Merriam-Webster, http://www.merriam
      -webster.com/dictionary/riff.

180   **While riffing is something:** Peter Meehan, "The Creative Life of
      Chefs René Redzepi and Daniel Patterson," *Food & Wine*, January
      2012, http://www.foodandwine.com/articles/the-creative
      -life-of-chefs-rene-redzepi-and-daniel-patterson.

182   **This brings to mind the concept:** The following sources were
      used for this passage:
      Andrew Eisele, "George Foreman: Fight-by-Fight Career Record,"
          About.com, http://boxing.about.com/od/records/a/foreman.htm.
      "George Foreman Becomes Oldest Heavyweight Champ," His-
          tory, http://www.history.com/this-day-in-history/george
          -foreman-becomes-oldest-heavyweight-champ.
      Arlene Weintraub, "George Foreman: Marketing Champ of the
          World," *Bloomberg Businessweek*, December 19, 2004, http://
          www.businessweek.com/stories/2004-12-19/george-foreman
          -marketing-champ-of-the-world.

184   **What I found:** Michael D. Watkins, "How Managers Become
      Leaders," *Harvard Business Review*, June 2012, http://hbr.org/
      2012/06/how-managers-become-leaders/ar/1.

185   **I have spent:** Roger L. Martin, *The Opposable Mind: Winning Through Integrative Thinking* (Boston: Harvard Business School, 2009).

186   **Martin wrote of these leaders:** Roger Martin, "Becoming an Integrative Thinker: The Keys to Success," *The Huffington Post*, December 17, 2007, http://www.huffingtonpost.com/roger-martin/becoming-an-integrative-t_b_77171.html.

187   **Your work is to keep:** Dillard, *The Writing Life.*

188   **Igor and Marko Pusenjak:** The following sources were used for this passage:

"App Store Metrics," 148Apps.biz, http://148apps.biz/app-store-metrics/.

"Doodle Jump Is Everywhere," CBSNews video, 2:17, July 8, 2010, http://www.cbsnews.com/video/watch/?id=6659734n.

"A Look at the Developers of Doodle Jump, Igor and Marko Pusenjak," Edible Apple, http://www.edibleapple.com/2010/04/08/a-look-at-the-developers-of-doodle-jump-igor-and-marko-pusenjak/.

Chris Stevens, *Appillionaires: Secrets from Developers Who Struck It Rich on the App Store* (Oxford, UK: Wiley, 2011).

191   **Or you could use:** The following sources were used for this passage:

Paul Brownfield, "Don't Like the Movie? Let's Talk About It," *The New York Times*, June 1, 2012, http://www.nytimes.com/2012/06/03/movies/joel-hodgson-on-mystery-science-theater-and-riffs.html?pagewanted=all.

"Joel Hodgson Answers," Slashdot, http://news.slashdot.org/story/08/01/25/1457218/joel-hodgson-answers.

"MST3K Top Ten Best Lines," YouTube video, 3:14, posted by "Andrew Dickman," June 19, 2007, http://www.youtube.com/watch?v=CCHgyEieSAQ.

"Mystery Science Theater 3000," IMDb, http://www.imdb.com/title/tt0094517/.

"Ten of the Best MST3K Clips," YouTube video, 2:24, posted by
    "Teashade," June 21, 2009, http://www.youtube.com/watch?
    v=9KDvAiM5OvA.

Chapter Ten: Vitalize

195 **Frank Thomas and Oliver Johnston:** The following sources were
    used for this passage:
    Frank and Ollie, directed by Theodore Thomas (1995; Burbank,
        CA: Walt Disney Educational Media Co., 2003), DVD.
    Wade Sampson, "Frank and Ollie: The Best of Friends," Mouse
        Planet, April 14, 2010, http://www.mouseplanet.com/9215/
        Frank_and_Ollie_The_Best_of_Friends.

202 **I found other kids:** Gina Kolata, "Power in Numbers," *The New
    York Times*, January 2, 2012, http://www.nytimes.com/2012/01/
    03/science/broad-institute-director-finds-power-in-numbers
    .html?emc=eta1.

203 **The Lunar Society of Birmingham:** The following sources were
    used for this passage:
    Jenny Uglow, *The Lunar Men: Five Friends Whose Curiosity
        Changed the World* (New York: Farrar, Straus & Giroux,
        2002).
    "Lunar Society of Birmingham," Scholarly Societies Project,
        http://www.scholarly-societies.org/history/1775lsb.html.

204 **Lunar interests were kaleidoscopic:** Jenny Uglow, "Lunar Soci-
    ety of Birmingham," Oxford Dictionary of National Biography,
    http://www.oxforddnb.com/public/themes/59/59220.html.

208 **Mira Kirshenbaum:** Mira Kirshenbaum, *The Emotional Energy
    Factor: The Secrets High-Energy People Use to Beat Emotional
    Fatigue* (New York: Delacorte, 2003).

210 **The Center for Mentoring Excellence:** Laura Micheli, "Think
    You Know More Than Your Boss? You Just Might," Center for

Mentoring Excellence, http://www.centerformentoringexcellence
.com/upload/Reverse_Mentoring.pdf.

212   **The wiring of the brain:** Joseph LeDoux, *The Emotional Brain:
      The Mysterious Underpinnings of Emotional Life* (New York: Si-
      mon & Schuster, 1996).

213   **We have a special brain system:** Rebecca Saxe, "How We Read
      Each Other's Minds," filmed July 2009, TED video, 16:55, posted
      September 2009, http://www.ted.com/talks/rebecca_saxe_how_
      brains_make_moral_judgments.html.

Afterword

219   **The first comes:** *Fitzcarraldo*, directed by Werner Herzog (Mu-
      nich, Germany: Werner Herzog Filmproduktion, 1982).

220   **The second thought comes:** David Remnick, "We Are Alive,"
      The New Yorker, July 30, 2012, http://www.newyorker.com/
      reporting/2012/07/30/120730fa_fact_remnick?currentPage=all.

Index